LEGENDS
the
Bengals
Cincinnati

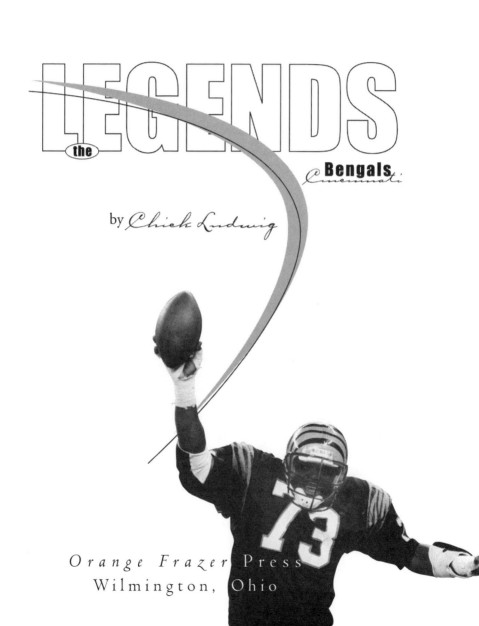

LEGENDS

the

Bengals
Cincinnati

by *Chick Ludwig*

Orange Frazer Press
Wilmington, Ohio

ISBN: 1-882203-38-0

Ordering information: Additional copies of *The Legends, Cincinnati Bengals:
the Men, the Deeds, the Consequences* may be ordered directly from:

Customer Service Department
Orange Frazer Press, Inc.
Box 214
37¹/2 West Main Street
Wilmington, Ohio 45177

Telephone 1-800-852-9332 for price and shipping information
Web site: www.orangefrazer.com

Library of Congress Cataloging-in-Publication Data

Ludwig, Chick, 1954-
    The legends : Cincinnati Bengals : the men, the deeds,
        the consequences / by Chick Ludwig.
        p. cm.
    ISBN 1-882203-38-0
        1. Cincinnati Bengals (Football team) 2. Football players--United States--
Biography. I. Title.

GV965.C54L83 2004
796.332'64'0977178--dc22

                                                            2004049518

Dedication

In memory of the 19 deceased Bengals players:
Doug Adams, linebacker, Ohio State, 1971-74; Jerry Anderson, safety, Oklahoma, 1977; Don Bass, wide receiver, Houston, 1978-81; Lewis Billups, cornerback, North Alabama, 1986-91; Bob Brown, defensive tackle, Arkansas A M&N, 1975-76; Frank Buncom, linebacker, Southern Cal, 1968; Steve Chomyszak, defensive tackle, Syracuse, 1968-73; Boobie Clark, running back, Bethune-Cookman, 1973-78; Jo-Jo Heath, safety/kickoff returner, Pittsburgh, 1980; Vernon Holland, offensive tackle, Tennessee State, 1971-79; Bernard Jackson, safety/kickoff returner, Washington State, 1972-76; Walter Johnson, defensive tackle, Los Angeles State, 1977; Bobby Kemp, safety, Cal State-Fullerton, 1981-86; Rufus Mayes, offensive tackle, Ohio State, 1970-78; Horst Muhlmann, placekicker, native of West Germany, 1969-74; Chip Myers, wide receiver, Northwestern Oklahoma, 1969-76; Nick Roman, defensive end, Ohio State, 1970-71; Brian Pillman, linebacker, Miami of Ohio, 1984; Wilson Whitley, defensive tackle, Houston, 1977-82.

Acknowledgements

To my parents, Chuck and Ruth; my siblings, Linda, Greg, Terri, Jeff, Dan and Barb; and my family, Peggy "Jo", Kelsie and Evan. Thank you for your guidance, love and friendship, and for allowing me to run this race. To my mentors and colleagues, past and present, at the *Dayton Daily News*, especially Si Burick, Ritter Collett, Patsy and Ralph Morrow, Hal McCoy, Gary Nuhn, Tom Archdeacon, Marty Williams, Bucky Albers, Mickey Davis, Dave Long, Marc Katz, Greg Simms, Leal Beattie, Skip Peterson, Steve Sidlo, Ray Marcano, Dwayne Bray, Jack Clary, John Murdough, Jerry Range, Peter King, Kevin Riley, and Frank Corsoe. Frank grudgingly OK'd my request for time off to finish this project. I appreciate his words of advice: "Shut up and write!" Thanks to Katie Blackburn and Eric Ball of the Bengals; the club's public relations staff of Jack Brennan, PJ Combs, and Inky Moore; Gary Langenbrunner, Dave Hermann, and Mike Botts of *Bengals Report* magazine; Erin Nedland of the NFL Players Association; and Steve Sabol and Patrick Pantano of NFL Films.

All helped me immensely. To the immortal Chick Evans, who founded the scholarship for golf caddies that allowed me to study journalism at The Ohio State University; and friends Bob Von Gries, Don and Marilyn Sullivan, Kevin O'Hearn, Ron Todd, Carlos Holmes, Jon Lesnik, Marla Ridenour, Marsha Bosley, Debbie Schoborg, Brenda Donald, Trish Brawner and Teri Moratschek, for their enthusiastic support of my career. The final thank you is reserved for the Bengals alumni, especially Dave Lapham, Isaac Curtis, Bob Johnson, Jim LeClair, John Stofa, Jim Breech, Lemar Parrish, and David Fulcher. I bludgeoned them with telephone calls and became a terrible nuisance, picking their brains for memories of teammates, and they never once complained. Curtis, "The Ice Man," is the alumni captain, the "go-to" guy everyone rallies around. He's total class. There was only one candidate to write the Legends' foreward—Lapham, Mr. Bengal. Emotion pours from his words, on the air and in print. He's a true prince in gym shoes. So is LeClair. As he signed off from our most recent conversation, LeClair spoke on behalf of all former Bengals players: "Don't forget us." Jim, you can rest assured, I never will.—*Chick Ludwig*

Picture credits—Unless otherwise listed, all photographs are from the *Dayton Daily News* archive, and their photographers are listed when known. Additional photography was provided by Chance Brockway of Columbus, Mike Botts/the *Bengals Report*, the Cincinnati Bengals, and many of the players themselves. Our immeasurable gratitude to all of them, and particularly to Skip Peterson of the *Dayton Daily News*.

Cover design by the inestimable Jeff Fulwiler

Contents

Prologue

The life of the shooter is a glamorous life. Travel, exotic climates, fascinating subjects. But do not take *our* word; listen to the professional shooter himself, out on such an assignment.

It is January 10, 1982, Riverfront Stadium, Cincinnati, Ohio. An exotic climate of 59 below zero—the coldest game in NFL history, if one takes wind chill into account, and on that day, everyone present surely did. It was the infamous Freezer Bowl, the workaday Bengals vs. those West Coast surf-and-turfers, the San Diego Chargers, playing for the AFC Championship and a trip to the Super Bowl.

Skip Peterson, *Dayton Daily News* photographer, was worried largely about what would happen if he fell down, wearing, as he was, snowmobile pants over a second pair of pants, sweats, sweater, and down vest. He felt like a *turtle*; if he went down, could he possibly rise again?

And there were worse problems: the cold condensed one's breath on the viewfinder, turning immediately to ice. To prevent that from happening, he had to hold his breath, wait for the moment, then shoot. All the while hoping that the picture revealed itself before he passed out from oxygen deprivation.

The cold made the film so brittle it sometimes broke inside the camera. *Good* luck meant that it broke at the beginning of a roll, rather than at the end. One simply poured the film out and began again. Changing film was an ordeal, too, because it meant removing one's gloves, whereupon the hands went numb.

So many members of the Fourth Estate sought refuge in the pressbox, management refused any more admittance. The photographers, resembling a rag-tag collection of Arctic explorers, huddled in the restroom for protection.

"At some point during the game," Peterson recalled, "it occurred to me that I simply could not become any colder. So I just forgot about it and went on with the work..."

He was most pleased with his photograph of Bengal quarterback Ken Anderson throwing the winning touchdown pass, his breath a frigid cloud of exhalation.

And that, sports fans, is the glamorous life.

When Chick Ludwig began his study of preeminent Bengals in franchise history, he quickly turned to the *Daily News*' photographic archives. The photo morgues of significant American newspapers are relatively unviewed collections containing thousands of images ranging from hopelessly mundane portraits of ribbon-cuttings to original moments of high drama. In other words, these images document our lives, and like our lives, they present a full expression, from the artificial to the art.

The *Daily News* sports archive, Ludwig found, was a museum, an exhibition of players at the apogee of their sporting lives. It was a splendid, almost unbroken chronicle of Bengaldom: Mike Reid at a piano. Ike Curtis chasing Benzoo, the mascot. Chip Myers trying to play his stereo with two broken arms. Anthony Munoz, a tousle-haired colossus rising amidst a gaggle of fans.

Clinging precariously to old dictums, Ludwig nonetheless considered the ratio too high: With *his* prose, perhaps it should take three, maybe *four* pictures to equal a thousand words. After reviewing the impressive *DDN* archive, that was the way he wanted it, anyway.

This, of course, brought a closer examination of the photographs: Who had done all this work, and how? The representative master, Ludwig felt, was Skip Peterson, the head of *DDN* photography, who had begun his career shooting the Bengals not long after the franchise arrived in Cincinnati.

Peterson's first Bengals game was an exhibition game in the late summer of 1972. He was a college intern from Bellbrook, Ohio, yet to finish Ohio University where he would be in the first class of university journalists to graduate with an emphasis in photojournalism. He was nervous on the elevator into Riverfront. *They* were professionals out there; would *he* be professional enough himself? Would the field be like, say, Colorado, where the air was rarified and he would need extra training to acclimate himself?

This insecurity, he found, lasted not much more than a quarter, and he soon made a miraculous discovery: The professional game was not much different from Friday night football in Bellbrook. The stadium was bigger. That was it.

As with all good photographers, Peterson learned where the competition was. It was between himself and the field, much as it was with the athletes themselves. Good photography, he would say, "is the extreme concentration resulting in that 1/1,000th moment in time which is the essence of the game. My job was to look for that intense moment of summation. There are a lot of good pictures out there. A blind person with an autofocus lens can make a good shot. But probably not a *great* shot..."

Herein, Peterson's photographs stand out, both action and portraiture, notable among them one of quarterback Boomer Esaison concentrating so fiercely downfield that the Houston linebacker clinging to his waist is a mere afterthought. This concentration is, too, the focus of the shooter.

"You're always looking for *the* picture," he says. "Friends tell me how lucky I am, that I get to see these great games, and I try to explain to them that I don't really watch the *game*. I work moment-to-moment, never thinking much about the score, or who is winning. And the photographer often plays like the team does: He has good days and bad days...."

Peterson shot the Bengals for over sixteen years. In that time, he may have worked as many as 150 games, and shot perhaps 50,000 frames. With Peterson are the other familiar bylines—Bill Waugh, Charlie Steinbrunner, Walt Kleine, Jim Rutledge, Bill Reinke, and the others. They go back to the era of two papers in Dayton and the origins of the franchise itself, having created a splendid photographic exhibit in which nearly four decades of both its gloom and its glory are compressed into, as Peterson himself said, "the moment in time which is the essence..."

Peterson does not shoot as much these days. He was never much of a fan, but now he goes with his wife to watch University of Dayton basketball games where he finds himself clinically observing. He still has trouble watching the game itself. "I find myself watching the floor, always, for the *picture*," he says.

Chick Ludwig's compilation of Bengal legends would be but half a book were it not for the revelation, grace, and sometimes surprising clarity of the images taken by Peterson and his fellow shooters.

–The editors

Foreword

Every child participating in youth football dreams about playing in the NFL. A very small percentage actually get to live that dream. I was one of the lucky ones and count my blessings every day. I guess that explains my passion for football at all levels. I loved my four years of high school football, earned a scholarship to Syracuse University, which led to twelve years of professional play.

I've been fortunate to broadcast high school, college, and professional football on radio and television, having loved every minute of it. Being drafted by Paul and Mike Brown in 1974 was the biggest day in my working life. I was proud to be a Cincinnati Bengal and I am proud to be a former Bengal—always have been; always will be.

Playing in Super Bowl XVI and broadcasting Super Bowl XXIII were experiences words can't describe. I've lived through seasons of incredible team accomplishment as well as struggle. But the common denominator through all those seasons was bonds formed among outstanding players and gifted coaches, all high-caliber individuals.

A tremendous source of pride for me is to see teammates who excel on the field during their football careers favorably impacting many other professional fields after their playing days are over. Having formed a lifelong friendship with the greatest Bengal of them all—Hall of Famer Anthony Munoz—is something I'll always cherish.

Boomer Esiason, Cris Collinsworth, Bob Trumpy, and Solomon Wilcots are outstanding broadcasting talents. Reggie Williams, Bob Johnson, Pat McInally, Isaac Curtis, and Max Montoya have all made statements in the business world. Mike Reid is as award-winning songwriter, musician, and singer. Tommy Casanova has made a huge contribution to medicine. Bruce Coslet, Ken Anderson, Tim Krumrie, Charlie Joiner, Chip Myers, Bruce Kozerski, and Mike Martin have made their mark in the coaching profession.

I've learned so much about football from the fertile minds of Bengal coaches like Sam Wyche, Bill Johnson, Jim McNally, Bill Walsh, Lindy Infante, Hank Bullough, and Dick LeBeau. My first head coach, Paul Brown, and my last head coach, Forrest Gregg, taught me lessons in life that I apply every day to this day. Marvin Lewis is so much more than just a football coach to his current Bengal players as well.

Chick Ludwig has a passion for football, too. He catches up with more than fifty former and current players and coaches. Some of the stories you probably have never heard before. The where-are-they-now and what-are-they-doing updates makes a terrific read. You'll thoroughly enjoy it. I know I did.

—*Dave Lapham, April, 2004*

College:
Buffalo
Hometown:
Johnstown,
Pennsylvania
Height: 6-3,
Weight:210

2

The Chosen One

¶John Stofa, quarterback (1968-'69)

And so it came to pass that on December 27, 1967, the Bengals—exactly three months after Paul Brown was awarded an American Football League franchise to begin play in 1968—got their first player. Brown went on a scouting mission to Miami, stood on the sidelines at a Dolphins' practice and watched the quarterbacks, especially John Stofa, rehabilitating from a fractured right ankle suffered in the 1967 season-opening 35-21 victory over Denver at the Orange Bowl.

As it turned out, Stofa's injury played a significant role in Dolphin history because his exit from the lineup launched the Hall of Fame career of quarterback Bob Griese, Miami's first-round draft pick in 1967.

"It's at the end of the '67 season. That's when Paul Brown comes down to Miami and we think he's looking at Rick Norton (the Dolphins' first-round draft pick from Kentucky in November 1965)," Stofa said.

"I'm over to the side doing my thing because I wasn't active. The next thing I know he's traded a first- and second-round draft choice to the Miami Dolphins for my services that next year. Apparently, he saw something he liked.

Stofa is one of only three quarterbacks—In the past 50 years—who has thrown a game-winning touchdown pass in the final minute of his first NFL start.

"I look back with a lot of pride that Paul Brown, a legend, was making John Stofa his first choice for the new franchise."

Stofa went undrafted out of the University of Buffalo in '64 and spent most of three years playing for the Daytona Beach Thunderbirds in the Southern Professional Football League, developing his arm in a pass-happy minor league comparable to today's Arena Football League.

Head coach George Wilson invited Stofa to Miami's first training camp in '66, and liked what he saw. But the Dolphins already had Dick Wood, George Wilson Jr., and Norton.

"I was having a pretty good camp," Stofa said. "But they had money invested in some other guys and Wilson said, 'I don't want to cut you, but I'm in a bind here.' "

Wilson got Stofa a tryout with the Pittsburgh Steelers, but he was released late in training camp. So he returned to Daytona Beach only to get re-signed by Miami, where he started—and made history—in the Dolphins' final game of their inaugural '66 season.

In the past 50 years, only three quarterbacks—Stofa, Buffalo's Frank Reich (1989) and Cincinnati's Akili Smith (1999)—have thrown game-winning touchdown passes in the final minute of their first NFL start. Stofa passed for four TDs, capped by a 14-yard strike to Joe Auer with 38 seconds remaining, for a 29-28 victory over the Houston Oilers in front of 20,045 spectators at the Orange Bowl.

He earned the starting job over Griese, Norton, and Jon Brittenum in '67, until fate intervened against the Broncos.

"We're in the tunnel, going out to play our first game that season, and I told Rick, 'I just feel so great. I'm going to have one heck of a game, and also a great season,'" Stofa said.

After Stofa's TD run gave Miami a 7-0 lead, his ankle snapped on the first play of the second series.

"I drop back and I'm going to throw a bomb down the middle," he said. "But somebody misses a block and now I'm trapped back there. I was spun around and my ankle stayed planted and I broke it." Three screws were inserted in Stofa's ankle and he was out for the year. Ironically, defensive end Pete Duranko—a Notre Dame great who was

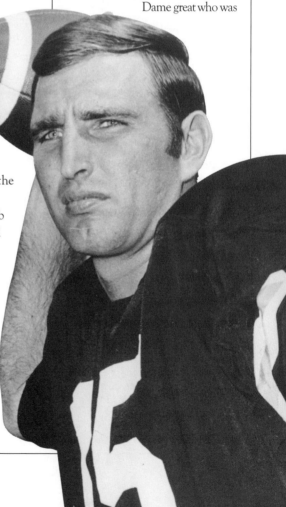

Stofa's teammate at Bishop McCort High School in Johnstown, Pennsylvania—was in on the tackle that changed Stofa's career.

That first training camp at Wilmington College resembled Grand Central Station. Players were flown in to Cincinnati and Columbus, then bused to Wilmington.

"I still remember the coaches going out to the bus station, welcoming two or three players, letting them get off the bus, run a 40-yard dash, then putting two of 'em back on the bus," Stofa said.

The expansion team struggled to a 3-11 record as Stofa completed 85 of 177 passes (48 percent) for 896 yards, threw five TDs and five interceptions. But he earned his place in franchise lore by being the first of 686 players to wear Bengals stripes. Stofa's most memorable game came at Miami on November 17, 1968, when he relieved an injured Sam Wyche

in the second quarter and engineered a 38-21 victory over his former team—including a 55-yard TD pass to Warren McVea.

Released in 1969 when rookie Greg Cook blossomed as the starter, Stofa was picked up by the Dolphins and traded in '71 to Denver.

"I think back to the Monday meetings and Paul critiquing the game and going over the films and he makes a statement like, 'Some of you guys did not play up to expectations and some of you guys aren't going to be here tomorrow.'

"All of a sudden you saw 45 heads in the room drop. *Nobody* wanted to make eye contact with him."

(Stofa, 62, has been working in the health insurance business for 20 years. He lives in the Columbus, Ohio, suburb of Blacklick and serves as vice-president of Medical Mutual. His hobbies are golf and fishing.)

> The coaches went out to the bus station, welcomed two or three players, had them run a 40-yard dash, then put two of 'em back on the bus.
>
> —John Stofa, on first Bengal camp

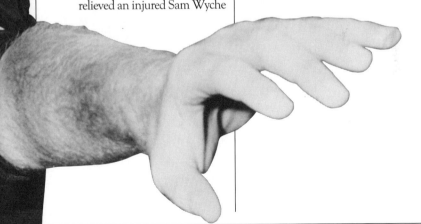

Center Stage

¶Bob Johnson, center (1968-'79)

Number 54 was retired in a halftime ceremony at Riverfront Stadium on December 17, 1978—a 48-16 victory over Cleveland. The club brought Bob Johnson and his family onto the field and thanked him for the memories, as well as 11 years of excellence as the offensive captain. "I couldn't have been more honored," said Johnson, the first draft pick of the AFL expansion franchise in 1968.

College: Tennessee
Hometown: Cleveland, Tennessee
Height: 6-5,
Weight: 261
Pro Bowls: 1

"At the same time, I was almost a little embarrassed. I'm the only guy to have his number retired, but other players deserved it. Being the first draft choice, I'm sure, had a lot to do with it."

All 46,985 spectators in attendance that day automatically assumed that was the last they'd seen of Johnson in a Bengals uniform. After all, he was ready to get on with his life's work in tackling the business world, an arena where he has excelled as everyone knew he would. But the Bengals called him back to duty and he responded, agreeing to be the long-snapper for the final six games of 1979.

He was at his office when the telephone rang. Assistant General Manager Mike Brown was on the line. "(Center) Blair Bush had hurt his knee and (guard) Max Montoya bounced and snapped the ball over (punter) Pat McInally's head," Johnson said. "Mike called me and said, 'Would you be willing to come back and snap?' I said, 'Mike, I can't just walk away from this.' He said, 'You don't have to practice. Just come out on Sundays and snap. I'm sure you remember how.'"

You betcha, he remembered.

Paul Brown made quarterback John Stofa the first Bengal on December 27, 1967. Now Brown needed a center. So he tapped Johnson, an All-American from Tennessee, as his top draft pick on January 30, 1968, and immediately installed him as the captain before the club's inaugural season.

It was a motley crew—41 draft picks over 17 rounds plus 39 players selected in the 1968 AFL Expansion Draft—that gathered on July 5 for the first training camp at Wilmington College. Johnson's job was to be the glue that held the team together.

"Johnson has the finesse of a ballet dancer and the power of a runaway freight car," said sportswriter Dick Forbes.

6

Chance Brockway

"I was the first guy drafted, so for an expansion team, it was like I was one of the few guys that probably knew he was going to make the team," Johnson said. "I walked in and Coach Brown made me the captain, but I was the captain of a strange, unusual collection of people.

"You had a huge number of rookies and a bunch of people who were made available in the expansion draft. If you look back at that group, there were some good players, but as you would expect, there were no really good players in the prime of their career. They were either at the tail end or were viewed as marginal."

Johnson played every offensive snap his first six years, finally exiting the lineup with a fractured left ankle at Houston on November 17, 1974. "A guy clipped me while I was covering a punt," Johnson said. "The guy fair caught the ball and as I'm slowing down, someone hit me dead smack in the middle of the back of my ankle. But they did call the clip. After the game, he runs up to Paul Brown and apologizes, saying, 'I'm really sorry for hitting Bob Johnson like that.' Paul Brown looked at him coldly and said, 'All you did was break his ankle.'"

But Johnson bounced back in 1975 and it wasn't until '78, when Blair Bush became a first-round draft pick, that the club thought about replacing him. Bookend tackles Rufus Mayes and Vernon Holland had been great additions to the line in 1970 and '71, respectively. But Johnson, the man in the middle, was the constant from Day One.

"There are not many guys like Bob," said Dewey Warren, a Bengals backup quarterback in '68 who played three years with Johnson in college at Tennessee. "We never had a bad snap. He was a guy who was very intelligent, made all the calls on our offensive line and was naturally an All-American, graduated in four years in engineering, and came from a great family. Not only was he smart, but he had a lot of talent. He was a great leader and great person with great character. That's why Cincinnati drafted him No. 1."

And that's why no other Bengal will ever wear number 54. "I feel like it's a previous life," Johnson said about his playing days. "Like I've been reincarnated here. Like I was a different person. But it was a great time."

(Johnson, 58, is president of the industrial division of Sovereign Specialty Chemicals, Inc., a developer and supplier of specialty adhesives, working out of the Cincinnati office. He's a licensed pilot who plays tennis and is a voracious reader of American history from the Civil War on back.)

The Essex Express

¶Essex Johnson, halfback (1968-'75)

Essex Johnson was a joy to behold for Bengals' fans because he had moves on top of moves. Like an Emmitt Smith, he was tough enough to run inside. Like a Barry Sanders, he had the stop-and-start quickness and acceleration that left defenders grabbing nothing but air as he breezed to the outside.

College: Grambling
Hometown: Shreveport, Louisiana
Height: 5-9, Weight:200

"I was a slashing runner," he said. "It was a no-nonsense kind of thing. The closest distance between two points is a straight line. I tried to go straight ahead, not with a lot of flair, but I could get the job done. I had good speed and that was one of the assets that helped me to overcome some of the size difference."

Johnson, of course, is being modest. He had a low center of gravity that allowed him to run low to the ground. He'd take a handoff and hide among the trees that were his offensive linemen, then pop out and burst downfield.

"When you see (Kansas City Chiefs kick returner) Dante Hall make those cuts and it looks like his butt's just inches off the ground, Essex could do that," Bengals guard Dave Lapham said. "He made a living hiding behind those big guys, then he'd explode on you.

"The other thing I remember about Essex is that he would plant and spin getting north and south. He'd be heading upfield, plant his left or right foot, and spin. He had the tightest spin move I've ever seen."

Slashing and dashing. Spinning and grinning. That was "The Essex Express." He said he opened up the sports section of *The Cincinnati Enquirer* one day, saw the nickname in print and it stuck.

Johnson sure stuck it to the San Diego Chargers on September 30, 1973. Operating behind a line that featured center Bob Johnson, guards Howard Fest and Pat Matson, and tackles Stan Walters and Vernon Holland, Essex became the first Cincinnati player to record 100 yards rushing and 100 yards receiving in the same game. He cranked out 121 yards on 21 carries and 116 yards on two receptions in a 20-13 Bengals victory. Johnson stood alone in that

Essex Johnson, one of the original Bengals—as well as perhaps the fastest—was known as "Mr. Big Play."

category until 1986 when James Brooks joined him.

"The sun was shining, I had a good surface to work with, and I was feeling good that day," Johnson said. "It just happened. You try to prepare for a good day everyday, but it depends on the people up front, too—how they're working and how the game plan is designed for the defense we are working against. Everybody was blocking. It was very balanced."

Johnson was a part of two expansion franchises. Picked by the Bengals in the sixth round of the 1968 AFL Draft, he played eight seasons in Cincinnati before shipping off to the 1976 expansion Tampa Bay Buccaneers. Ohio State's Heisman Trophy winner, Archie Griffin, came aboard as a Bengals' first-round draft pick in '76 and there was no longer room for two small but mighty tailbacks.

Johnson played for the Bucs during their inaugural 0-14 season, then retired, leaving behind a career portfolio that included 112 games played, 3,236 yards rushing (a 4.5 average), 1,742 yards receiving (an 11.9 average) and 31 touchdowns—5.7 yards every time he touched the ball.

"Looking back, I was able to avoid the big hits put on me and my career was lengthened because of it," he said. "I appreciate my linemen because you've got to have those big boys up front doing work for you. My career was longer than what I could have ever expected."

(Johnson, 58, is a real estate developer who owns the Essex Realty company in Inglewood, California. "I still play tennis," he said, "but that's about the extent of it.")

Jim Rutledge

Essex rarely took a slobber-knocker hit. He made 'em miss. It was always a glancing type blow.

—Dave Lapham

13

Cinder(f)ella Story

¶Paul Robinson, halfback (1968-'72)

Before he became the first 1,000-yard rusher in club history, Paul Robinson didn't know the Cincinnati Bengals existed. He had no idea the American Football League had awarded the city a franchise. So you can imagine his surprise when he walked into the University of Arizona athletic department one fine day in March 1968. "The coaches told me, 'There's going to be a team called the Cincinnati Bengals and you just got drafted in the third round,'" Robinson said. "I couldn't believe it. I thought they were lying."

College:
Arizona
Hometown:
Marana,
Arizona
Height: 6-0,
Weight: 198
Pro Bowls: 2

But a letter of confirmation arrived from Paul Brown, and Robinson and his wife were thrilled with the summons to Cincinnati and just a little panicky when their plane landed at Greater Cincinnati Airport in Northern Kentucky.

"We flew in there and we were lost because we thought we were in Ohio," he said. "We took a cab to the Netherland Hilton. We didn't even know how to get on the elevator to go up to our floor. We were on the 12th or 13th floor, and we'd never been that high in our life. We were up in this big old hotel, looking out and saw those little cars. We locked the window and got away from it. We made sure we didn't fall out."

Robinson's story is amazing, considering how he started and where he ended. He played one season of college ball, scored the first touchdown

in Bengals history on September 6, 1968, with a 2-yard run in a Friday night game at San Diego and became AFL Rookie of the Year with a league-leading 1,023 rushing yards.

Although Robinson's signature play was the sweep, his 87-yard TD burst off right tackle at Oakland on October 27, 1968—thanks to the blocking of center Bob Johnson, guard Pat Matson, and tackle Howard Fest—stood as the longest rushing play in franchise history for 33 years until Corey Dillon's 96-yarder at Detroit on October 28, 2001.

Traded to Houston after the '72 season, Robinson spent two years with the Oilers before jumping to the Birmingham Americans of the World

Robinson was a basketball player and track star—"the Cactus Comet"—who used a fifth year of eligibility at Arizona to try football for the first time.

Chance Brockway

That 87-yard run was a '24' play. I ran off tackle, cut to the right, and I was on my way, baby.

—Paul Robinson

Football League. Like most of his "Ams" teammates, Robinson is still waiting for the World Bowl Championship ring he earned, but never received because of the club's financial demise.

Robinson was just a poor country kid from a small town outside Tucson. He played basketball at Eastern Arizona Junior College, ran track at Arizona, then used a fifth year of eligibility to play football.

He caught the Bengals' eye when the Wildcats upset Ohio State, 14-7, in 1967 at Columbus. "The only thing I wanted to do was make Arizona's team, which I did," Robinson said. "I was just a backup running back, handling kickoffs and punt returns, when we went to Ohio State. But the starting running back

got hurt and they put me in. Someone from the Bengals was at that Ohio State game and saw me. Whatever I did that day, it must've been good enough."

The Robinsons' flight to Cincinnati was harrowing, but their meeting with Paul Brown the following day was humbling. "We were surprised because you see the legend, Paul Brown, on TV and in newspapers, but in person, he was real little," Robinson said.

"I thought he was going to be 6-foot-10 and just so big he can't get through the door. He was sitting there and we thought he was the office manager or something like that. He's observing us. Me and my little wife were

18

talking. We look at this guy and he just stared at us. And then all of a sudden he said, 'My name is Paul Brown.'

"Oh, man, shoot, it took us a whole minute to look and say, God, this is Paul Brown. I told him, 'Sir, I'm just so glad to meet you, but you really don't look like the man I anticipated.'

"He said, 'This is what we're going to give you—a $15,000 bonus and a $15,000 regular-season salary. Take it or leave it.' Well, $15,000, when you don't have nuthin', that's a million dollars to us. We signed for that."

Being so far away from home for the first time, Robinson was petrified during that first training camp at Wilmington College. "Every morning at 6 o'clock, there would be a knock on the door, and the key words were: 'Paul Brown wants to see you and bring your playbook.' So every day, I would call home and say, 'I'll be home.' You'd hear a knock on the door and I'd tell my roommate, 'Well, nice meeting you. This is for me.' But they kept calling the other guy."

As a high hurdler, he knew it was critical to get a fast start. His technique was to beat everyone to the first hurdle. His philosophy in football was the same—hit the hole quickly and don't fumble. During the intrasquad scrimmage, Robinson ripped off runs of 20 and 30 yards before Brown told him to take a seat.

"That was the first time the news media came up to me. They said I did this and that. Who are you and where are you from? I told 'em: 'If I make the team, I'm going to be rookie of the year.' That was my goal."

Robinson likes to tell people that the first time he saw a professional game in person was the one he got to start in—an August 3, 1968, exhibition against the Kansas City Chiefs at Nippert Stadium.

"As a running back, you do not look at the hole," Robinson said, "because the defense is looking at your eyes. Man, I kind of glanced at my hole and I could just see big Buck Buchanan of the Chiefs staring at me...."

Slowed by ankle and knee injuries during his career, he played in 79 games over seven NFL seasons, rushed 737 times for 2,947 yards (a 4.0 average) and 24 TDs, and caught 90 passes for 612 yards and two scores. One day, he would like to attend a game at Paul Brown Stadium and see the mural of himself that adorns one of the entrances. It's a fitting tribute to a man who rose off the Arizona cinders to become a Bengals legend.

(Robinson, 60, is a Graham County juvenile probation officer in Safford, Arizona, two hours east of Tucson. His hobbies are basketball and jogging.)

Mr. Cool Breeze

¶Bob Trumpy, tight end (1968-'77)

Every Bengals player who ever survived a training camp, from 1970 on, owes Bob Trumpy a huge debt of gratitude. Because of his enterprising skill and public-relations savvy, he ensured that all players stayed cool once they climbed out of summer's oven. He got 'em the forbidden fruit of air conditioning. Trumpy and his roommate, Bob Johnson, plucked ol' "Betsy"—a noisy, heavy, wood-framed air conditioner—from the attic of Melna Burchenal's Glendale home prior to 1969 training camp, stuck it in the window of their Wilmington College dormitory room, and told everybody it was an "air cooler."

College: Utah
Hometown:
Springfield,
Illinois
Height: 6-6,
Weight:228
Pro Bowls: 4

One problem: There was barely enough electricity to handle the power surge, so when the compressor kicked on, the lights in all the dorm rooms dimmed. "The maintenance guy runs down to Paul Brown and says, 'Somebody's got an air conditioner. You better get rid of it,'" Johnson said.

"Coach Brown walks up and Trumpy goes into this diatribe: 'Coach Brown, we got this out of Melna Burchenal's attic. This is an air cooler, not an air conditioner. About that time, the compressor hits and dims the lights. Coach Brown has this little mousy smile on his face and says, 'OK,' and leaves. The next year, everybody had air conditioners."

The key here was Burchenal, now 72. She was a friend of PB's who threw lavish parties for the coaches. Johnson and Trumpy always showed up the next day to devour the leftovers.

That's what Trumpy was supposed to be, a leftover, ready to be discarded, when he was picked in the 12th round (301st overall) in the AFL Draft. One of 23 receivers fighting for five spots at camp, Trumpy made the squad because he was the most versatile receiver on the club.

The "Longshot Legend" survived 10 years, making four trips to the Pro Bowl and piling up 298 catches for 4,600 yards (a 15.4 average) and 35 TDs in 128 games.

To understand how he did it, you have to go back to the spring of '68 in

Trumpy became the only pro player to be drafted out of the Beneficial Finance Corporation— thus going from longshot to NFL bigshot.

6 The thing to remember about me is I could get deep. I could outrun most of the safeties that played the game in those days.

—Bob Trumpy

Skip Peterson

21

California. Fresh out of Utah, Trumpy quit his job with a collection agency when a gun got aimed at him on a porch in Compton. His new job, building Shasta Travel Trailers, required heavy lifting, which kept him in shape.

Driving past the campus of San Fernando Valley State College on his way home from work, he noticed some football players working out. He stopped and asked if he could join in because he had just been drafted by the Bengals.

"The next day, as I approach the field, I notice a bag on the ground from the Green Bay Packers," Trumpy said. "Lo and behold, that bag belonged to Zeke Bratkowski, who lived in Sherman Oaks, another valley community.

"For the next three and a half months, four days a week, I worked out with Zeke and several other guys, so when I came into camp, I was in the best shape of my life. He taught me things about playing the position that the Packers did.

"When we finally broke up and he was going to Green Bay and I was going to Cincinnati, he said: 'Look, Trumpy, I'm going to mention your name to our coaching staff. We could use you. We need big receivers. You can play inside or outside for us. If you get cut, don't be surprised if you get a call from the Packers.'

"Nobody to this point in my life had ever been that complimentary about my athletic skills. I figured if Zeke Bratkowski, the backup to (Hall of Famer) Bart Starr, thinks I can make it, hell, I can make it. I went to camp with that attitude. I've always thanked Zeke for that."

Courtesy of Bengals offensive coordinator Bill Walsh, Trumpy blossomed into a star because of how he was used. He was a tight end with wide receiver speed, and Walsh moved him around, creating mismatches against befuddled defensive backs.

"What he was trying to do was put me on the free safety of other teams, so we flopped the tight end," Trumpy said. "We were the first team in the NFL to move the tight end around. Bill had to call the league office to find out what was allowed and what wasn't.

"Paul didn't like it because when the tight end moved, he said, it looked like we didn't know where to line up. But we started using it and we blew defenses away because I could get deep. Opponents had a real choice to make—either put a real coverage guy on me and lose a tackler or put a centerfielder (free safety) on me and I could beat 'em all to death."

Trumpy caught the Bengals' first TD pass at Nippert Stadium—a 58-yarder from John Stofa at 8:58 of the

Bill Shepherd

I was Trumpy's roommate and the only thing I can say about him is: He and I never agreed on anything. But he wasn't boring. So I could have predicted his success as sports talk show host.

—Bob Johnson

"Apologies? Absolutely none. I never hid from the criticism I put on the franchise. If Paul had anything to say to me, I was going to be right there so he could say it to me. I wasn't going to be quiet.

—Bob Trumpy

third quarter in a 24-10 victory over Denver on September 15, 1968. He also had three TD receptions in a 31-all tie at the Houston Astrodome on November 9, 1969—the only tie in franchise history.

But Trumpy's most memorable game was a 23-17 victory over Miami on November 20, 1977. In a driving rainstorm at Riverfront Stadium, he caught a 29-yard TD pass from quarterback Ken Anderson on a flea flicker that knocked the Dolphins out of the playoffs. The play still eats at Dolphins' Hall of Fame coach Don Shula.

...Anderson hands off to halfback Archie Griffin. Griffin dishes to wide receiver John McDaniel. McDaniel hands it back to Anderson, who throws it to Trumpy...touchdown Bengals!

"It was magic," Trumpy said. "Don Shula reminds me of that play every time I see him. We called it 'triple pass' because three people touched it before I caught it, but Shula called it the reverse pass. He never stops. He'll see me and say: 'That damn reverse pass. I remember that.'"

(Trumpy, 59, is a nationally-known broadcaster who serves as the analyst for Sunday night NFL games on CBS Radio Sports/Westwood One and does a variety of programming for WLW-AM (700) radio. "I play golf, am a serious fisherman, and I love building furniture in the workshop I have in the back of my property.")

Eddie Roberts

Monster in the Middle

¶Bill Bergey, middle linebacker (1969-'73)

He has two sons who play professional lacrosse. And if Jake and Josh Bergey are anything like their old man, then mud, blood, pain, and pride are among their closest friends. Bill Bergey knew all four well. He also knew what it was like to get on Paul Brown's bad side. Cross the line and there's no turning back. Bergey played brilliantly for five seasons in Cincinnati until the mother of all falling-outs took place and he got traded away to Philadelphia where he became an icon. But he left behind a legacy in the Queen City as the baddest, meanest, and toughest middle linebacker in club history.

College: Arkansas State
Hometown: South Dayton, New York
Height: 6-2,
Weight: 243
Pro Bowls: 1

"My style was just all-out," he said. "I never slowed for anything. That way you don't get hurt. I was an oversized linebacker for the time and I had real good speed. The thing that probably helped me more than anything is I could run laterally as fast as I could run straight ahead."

Bengals guard Guy Dennis, Bergey's roommate and best friend, said he's never seen a more intense player than Bergey. "Bergey was crazy," Dennis said. "He'd make the All-Madden team. He was toughness and intensity put together. He was a different person when he took the field. He just changed. His eyes lit up and he was ready to kill or be killed. It was just remarkable to see."

On November 2, 1969, Bergey, a rookie second-round draft pick, was ready to kill. The Bengals crushed Oakland, 31-17, at Nippert Stadium, handing the 12-1-1 Raiders their only regular-season loss. The mission that day was to neutralize Raiders' center Jim Otto, who became a Hall of Famer.

"I had watched film on Jim Otto and I just thought he was the greatest guy as far as a player goes because he never made a mistake," Bergey said. "Everybody he was supposed to block he blocked. So I went into the game thinking if I can just make a couple of tackles that'll be more than anybody else had done. I got into this game and I was on fire. I must've had 20 tackles. I can remember Greg Cook coming off the bench one time, running onto the field and high-fiving

Bergey was an instrumental part of the Bengals' first playoff team; it was three years old and no team then had made the playoffs so quickly.

26

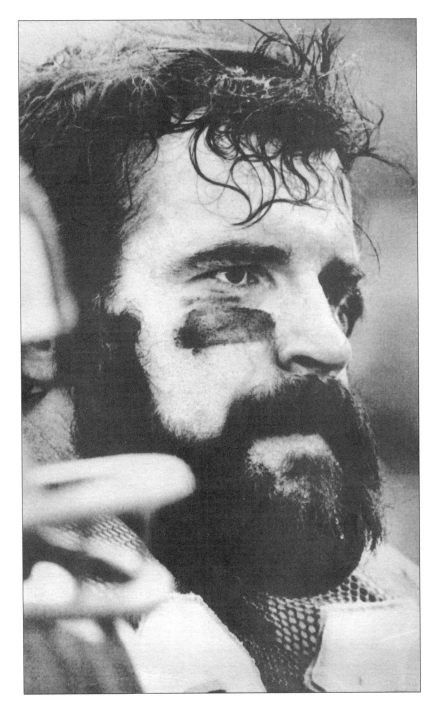

27

me because I was in such a groove." Bergey was credited with 10 solo tackles and four assists that day.

"They shortchanged me because I was all over the damn place," he said. He still remembers his interception against Bart Starr that he returned for a TD in a 10-10 tie at Green Bay in a 1970 preseason game. "It was an exhibition game, but to me it still counted," he said.

"Vince Costello, my linebackers coach, said, 'Good news and bad news. Good news is you intercepted the ball and we got a tie out of the game. The bad news is you were so far out of position when you caught the ball that Bart Starr will never know what coverage we were in.'"

What a season that turned out to be. With 60,157 fans in full throat on December 20, 1970, Bergey and safety John Guillory hoisted Paul Brown on their shoulders and carried him off the field after a 45-7 victory over the Boston Patriots at Riverfront Stadium. The triumph clinched a playoff berth for the three-year-old franchise. At the time, no other team had reached the playoffs so early in their history.

The good times were rolling, but nobody was laughing about the futures contract Bergey signed with the World Football League Virginia Ambassadors after the '73 season that led to a bitter court battle and his trade to the Eagles. Bergey intended to play the final year

of his Bengals contract in '74, then jump to the WFL. Although he won the battle in U.S. District Court, he lost his job in Cincinnati because he crossed Paul Brown.

"I was a young guy, married and had a kid, and I was making my move simply based on economics," Bergey said. "I love Cincinnati. I love my five years there. I have a lot of friends in Cincinnati. Paul Brown got me started in my life's work.

"But when this new league came along and they offered me between five and six times the amount of money I was making and I was going to get more than a two-year salary in just a bonus, that's when you have to take a good, hard look."

The Bengals, of course, saw it differently. "He was under contract to us and he signed a contract to play out in the future with the World Football League," Mike Brown said. "Our argument was you can't answer to two masters. Fine, if you wanted to sign with somebody, wait until his contract ended and his obligation to perform ended, then do it. Don't do it while he's still under obligation.

"He won that. We thought a strong federal judge might have the gumption to not make our district, our circuit, follow that law. But the judge here chose to follow the basketball precedent and we lost the case. We had Jim LeClair, and so we traded Bergey. Having said all that, Bill Bergey was the best linebacker this team ever had."

Before Bergey ever played a down in the WFL, the league bombed. He wanted to get back into the NFL. "But I had already crossed Paul Brown," he said. "It was very obvious that there was no way I was going to play on this team."

On July 10, 1974, Bergey was traded for three draft picks—a No. 1 in '77 and a first- and second-rounder in '78. Coupled with the trade of Coy Bacon and Lemar Parrish to Washington following the '77 season, the Bengals were able to secure five first-round picks in a two-year span. They drafted Eddie Edwards and Wilson Whitley in '77 and Ross Browner in '78, a trio that formed the famed "WEB" defensive line. Bergey played seven years for the Eagles (1974-80) and the big, burly linebacker remains a legend in both NFL cities.

(Bergey, 59, is the analyst on Eagles radio broadcasts for flagship station WYSP-FM–94.1. He's also part of a group in Philadelphia that invests in hotels, golf courses, and apartment complexes. "Fishing is my passion," he says. "Every year, my high school buddies go to northern Quebec. We're up there 10 days with walleye and northern pike, and it's unbelievable.")

The Cincinnati Kid

¶Greg Cook, quarterback (1969-'74)

College:
Cincinnati
Hometown:
Chillicothe,
Ohio
Height: 6-4,
Weight:215

At a corner table over lunch at his favorite Cincinnati hangout, Weber's Cafe, Greg Cook stabbed at his steak and opened an old wound. Injuries that happen 35 years ago are supposed to fade in the mist of history, but this one will forever be fresh and mysterious. When Cook's right shoulder exploded on a tackle at Nippert Stadium on September 28, 1969, in a 24-19 victory over the eventual Super Bowl IV champion Kansas City Chiefs—further damage was suffered in a pickup basketball game in the 1970 preseason—the course of Bengals' history changed. Not only would the injury wreck his marriage, it robbed him of what many believe would have been a Hall of Fame career, and cost the Bengals one, if not multiple, Super Bowls.

The cool, cocky, charismatic gunslinger was that good. So good that he earned All-America honors at UC in 1968 by leading the nation in passing yards (3,272) and touchdowns (25). So good that he was picked No. 5 overall in the 1969 American Football League Draft. So good that, despite the injury, he came back after missing four games to upset Oakland and finish the most storied rookie season for a quarterback in club history. So good that Hall of Fame coach Bill Walsh, who was a Bengals assistant from 1968-75, called him "the greatest talent I've ever seen at the quarterback position."

The club finished 4-9-1, but Cook led the AFL in passing, completing 106 of 197 passes for 1,854 yards, 15 touchdowns, and 11 interceptions for an AFL-high and single-season franchise record 9.41-yards-per-attempt average, and an 88.3 passer rating that ranks second in pro football history among rookies behind Dan Marino

UC's Dick MacPherson, who recruited him, called him Mr. Everything. "Handsome, talented, a natural leader, he was one of those great athletes who come along. He had it all."

(96.0). He threw to the backs (Paul Robinson and Jess Phillips), the wide receivers (Eric Crabtree, Speedy Thomas, and Chip Myers) and had a special bond with tight end Bob Trumpy, who would split out and abuse safeties with his size and speed— all with plays designed by Walsh, whom Cook credits with his success.

"We got out of the blocks really quickly," Cook said, "and we got a running start. For a second-year franchise, we were really on a winning tangent. I was able to throw the ball to a lot of people, and we attacked defenses where they weren't. That's really the concept of the West Coast offense."

Then, suddenly, a career that began with so much promise was extinguished by an injury that would be easily correctable by arthroscopic surgery in today's high-tech world.

"What do I want fans to think when they hear my name? It's hard to answer," Cook said. "I wanted the respect of what I did, but I didn't do much because I wasn't there for a long period. My greatest frustration, and it was a frustration— not a psychological trauma—is that I wish I could have played a full career.

"The first couple of years, after the injuries, it was more frustrating then. But you get to the point where age takes care of everything."

What we know is that Cook endured three surgeries in an attempt to repair a ripped rotator cuff and torn biceps tendon. He played in only one more game, completing one of three passes for 11 yards in 1973, and turned into one of those "what-could-have-been" legends.

What we don't know is exactly who is responsible for causing Cook's cannon arm to go silent. To this day, it's shrouded in mystery. Cook said NFL Films claimed the injury came on an open-field tackle. One historian said it occurred on a sack by Hall of Fame linebacker Willie Lanier. Other reports say Cook was hit by Jerry Mays and Bobby Bell. Cook said the injury came in the third quarter on a play in front of the Bengals' bench.

"It was on a roll-out," he said. "I threw the ball and got tripped, and I threw my hands out as you do when you trip forward to catch yourself. Two guys fell on the back of me, speared my shoulder and the way I fell, and all that weight, just tore the rotator cuff and tore my biceps tendon out a little bit, too. I thought I had dislocated it, but I didn't know the terminology. I just knew something was wrong."

Of Cook, Mike Brown said, "He would have been a Hall of Fame player and we would have won more than one Super Bowl with him as the quarterback. He was a phenomenon. He was a faster-developing John Elway."

He was the greatest talent I've ever seen at the QB position.

—Bill Walsh

James Rutledge

Cook had just been named the AFL's Back of the Week after throwing for 327 yards and three TDs, plus rushing for a score in a 34-20 victory over San Diego, prompting Chargers coach Sid Gillman to tell Bengals business manager John Murdough, "You've got the greatest-looking quarterback I've seen in a long time. You can go a long way with him."

Cook downplays the pickup basketball game—which came as the Bengals prepared to open Riverfront Stadium to a public excited by the NFL-AFL merger—but Murdough doesn't. "When Sid Gillman says a quarterback is great, he's great," Murdough said. "The club was built around him. He was doing a great job and then he got that injury. There's always some question about it.

"He got hurt in a football game, but he was up at UC a lot, and got in a pickup basketball game. Greg was going in for a shot and a guy grabbed his arm, held him and that's when he hurt his right arm. He had been injured, but really messed it up then."

The first operation took place the summer of 1970 at Cleveland Clinic. Two more surgeries followed and it wasn't until the third procedure, according to Cook, that the torn biceps tendon was discovered and reattached.

"How we did it, the comebacks

James Rutledge

34

and how the injury was attended to, was—at that time—the only way you could really do it. Unfortunately, you have to wait six to eight weeks to do anything after a surgical procedure. You had three operations and a two-month period after each one of them. It really delayed any kind of comeback."

The rotator cuff may have been healed, but the great amount of scar tissue caused inflammation in the shoulder muscles every time he threw. The stress on his arm was too much to bear.

The end finally came on July 15, 1974, a Monday morning, when Cook bolted training camp at Wilmington College. He left behind a note: "I can't do it anymore."

The following July, he was claimed off waivers by Kansas City, but never played. "Let me be perfectly frank," Cook said. "People remember you far more gracefully or better than you really were. It's almost like if a woman had to remember how it felt to deliver a child, she'd never have another child. So the pain in these people's minds about 'what-could-have-been' enhances what really was.

"I've always said, 'Sometimes you become more famous in your absence.' When you're gone, people remember you, and your performances are much more enhanced than they probably really were."

Through all the failed comeback attempts, there was one constant for Cook. His artwork. He had been a fine arts major at UC, and found escape in his portraits and landscape paintings. He couldn't erase his past, but with a stroke of a brush, he could change his future.

"My art, my personality will go the rest of my life," he said. "Football was temporary. I do suffer the scars of those years, but I'm probably as good a person, in my own mind, and I think probably to a lot of other people, than maybe I would have been."

"The memory of his long hair, modish clothes, sports car, his breezy self-confidence, and his availability to be interviewed or to sign autographs would last for awhile," Ritter Collett once wrote, "but the magic in his throwing arm was gone."

True. But the Cincinnati Kid will never be forgotten.

(Cook, 57, spent 18 years selling industrial chemicals. He and two friends have started a logging company, Queen City Wood Products, contracting with landowners in the Tri-State area. Despite his arthritic shoulder, he still participates in charity golf events, but his passion is painting. Cook is single.
"I think probably too many gals have suffered from my psychological setbacks, if you will.")

> The offensive linemen played touch football every Tuesday morning after film. When Greg came, he'd say, 'This is too easy.' So he backed up 15 or 20 yards and threw the ball 40 yards instead of 20. He just had a real gun.
>
> —Bob Johnson

Mr. Third Down

¶Chip Myers, wide receiver (1969-'76)

Instead of a helmet, shoulder pads, and cleats, Chip Myers should've brought a lunch pail, hard hat, and work boots to games. He did all the dirty work as a wide receiver for the Bengals for eight seasons, constantly coming through in the clutch on third down. Myers was your classic possession receiver—a huge target who was fearless coming across the middle against head-hunting defensive backs. In 108 career games, he caught 220 passes for 3,092 yards and 12 touchdowns, and was rewarded by his peers with a trip to the Pro Bowl in 1972.

College:
Northwestern
Oklahoma
State
Hometown:
Stillwater,
Oklahoma
Height: 6-6,
Weight: 205
Pro Bowls: 1

"He was that West Coast-offense control receiver like San Francisco's Dwight Clark, who everybody knew from The Catch against Dallas (in the 1982 NFC Championship game)," quarterback Virgil Carter said. "Chip ran those patterns where he'd be clearing through the middle from the off-side. You always knew where he was. He was steady, dependable, and very reliable."

On August 28, 1971, in a 22-21 preseason victory over the St. Louis Cardinals at Riverfront Stadium, Myers dived for a ball on the concrete-like AstroTurf and broke radius bones at the elbow in both arms. He was supposed to be out for six games. He missed only four.

You want tough?

You want Myers.

"I've often thought about going back and looking at the passing situations when Chip was thrown the ball," safety Tommy Casanova said. "I'll bet you over 75 percent of them were on third down and over the middle.

"He was not flashy, but he was the toughest, most dedicated guy. He was sort of gangly to look at, but he was a great athlete. He was a great pole

After breaking both arms (right), the casual Myers came back to catch 57 passes for 792 yards and an appearance in the Pro Bowl.

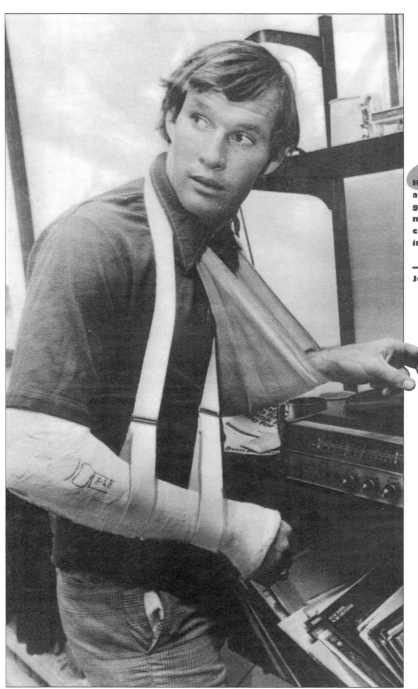

> He was a tough guy who made catches in crowds.
>
> —Bob Johnson

37

vaulter, a great skier, a great tennis player. Everything he did, he was good at. And he was like a big brother to me."

A 10th-round draft pick of the 49ers in 1967, Myers landed in Cincinnati as a free agent in '69 and led the team in receptions in '70, '72 and '74. Playing in the shadows of Eric Crabtree, Speedy Thomas, Isaac Curtis, Charlie Joiner, and Billy Brooks, Myers developed a reputation as one of the NFL's best clutch receivers, despite instability at quarterback early in his career.

"Some of Chip's best years were when we didn't have Kenny Anderson in his prime," center Bob Johnson said. "You go back to his first few years, there were a bunch of different quarterbacks, then Kenny came in relatively green. So Chip lost a few years.

"He wasn't Boyd Dowler because he wasn't as fast as somebody like Boyd Dowler, but he was big and deceptively fast. He had good speed and very good hands. He was a tough guy who'd make catches in crowds."

Strongly influenced by Hall of Fame coaches Paul Brown and Bill Walsh, Myers took to coaching naturally because of his communication skills and desire to teach. He was a full-time assistant for the Tampa Bay Buccaneers (1984), Indianapolis Colts (1985-88), New York Jets (1990-93) and New Orleans Saints (1994) before landing with the Minnesota Vikings.

Unflappable, easy-going and California cool, Myers coached the Vikings receivers from 1995-97, shifted to quarterbacks in '98 and was promoted to offensive coordinator by then-head coach Dennis Green in 1999, after Brian Billick left to become head coach of the Baltimore Ravens.

"My No. 1 goal when I came here was to stay a long time," Myers, an avid outdoorsman, told Vikings beat writers at the time. "It's a great place to live and a wonderful place to coach. I have my own ice house, so everything is great."

Myers had just returned from the 1999 NFL Scouting Combine in Indianapolis—where he spent time with his best friend, ex-Bengals teammate Bruce Coslet, and got a hug from Walsh, the 49ers' general manager at the time—when the unthinkable happened.

(Myers died of a heart attack in 1999, at his home in Long Lake, Minnesota. He was 53, survived by his wife and five children. "I don't think there was anybody in this building who was loved more than he was," ex-Vikings defensive coordinator Foge Fazio said.)

Myers hangs on to a Ken Anderson pass in an October 1975 meeting with New England, which the Bengals won 27-10, on their way to the divisional playoffs.

Skip Peterson

39

Master Thief

¶Ken Riley, cornerback (1969-'83)

Ken Riley was the consummate team player—totally unselfish, extremely classy and a model of consistency. His moniker, "The Rattler," was appropriate because it's taken from the nickname of his college in Tallahassee and it describes his playing style. For 15 years, his moves on the field were snake-smooth. And when it came to tracking the football in the air, tackling wide receivers and intercepting quarterbacks, he showed his fangs.

College: Florida A&M

Hometown: Bartow, Florida

Height: 6-0, Weight:186

Riley stole more passes than any Bengal, piling up 65, which ranks fifth in NFL history behind Paul Krause (81), Emlen Tunnell (79), Rod Woodson (71), and Dick "Night Train" Lane (68). Yet he never once got voted to the Pro Bowl and that's what's keeping him out of the Pro Football Hall of Fame.

While his flamboyant teammate, left corner-back Lemar Parrish, garnered headlines and six Pro Bowls, Riley quietly went about his business as the league's most consistent right cornerback.

There were only three years in which he had fewer than three

interceptions, and his 65 thefts, five INT returns for TDs and 596 interception-return yards are club records that may never be broken.

"Lemar was the Willie Mays and I was the Hank Aaron," Riley said. "I wasn't flashy. I wasn't a gambler, but I took advantage of situations. I believed in being in the right place. If you've got your technique down, good things happen. A lot of people underestimated my speed. I was faster than most people thought I was. And I was always quick."

Riley, who possessed great hands and concentration, was a scrambling quarterback at Florida A & M, where he earned his team's Scholastic award along with a Rhodes Scholar candidacy. He wanted a chance to

Riley never played like a rookie, even when he was one; he had four picks as a freshman, including one for 66 yards, and averaged 23.9 yards on kickoff returns.

Skip Peterson

40

> Ken was really good at timing his hits and spinning guys. We loved seeing guys flip. If they caught the ball, they had to pay for it.
>
> —Lemar Parrish

play quarterback in the NFL. But when he arrived in Cincinnati as a sixth-round draft pick in 1969, Paul Brown had other ideas.

"When I got there, Paul Brown said, 'You're a cornerback,' and that was it. I was used to backpedaling, scrambling, and changing directions. I had good peripheral vision. All those were attributed to my background as a quarterback. (Defensive coordinator) Tom Bass was the one who really got me off to a good start. I developed good fundamentals. I didn't have any bad habits."

He and Parrish kept a notebook on their enemies—"The do's and don'ts," Riley said—and they studied their nuances and intricacies. "Over a period of time, that notebook really helped me become the player I was."

Riley didn't play like a rookie in '69: he had four picks, including a personal-best 66-yarder, and averaged 23.9 yards on 14 kickoff returns. Fast forward to his final year in 1983 when he had eight interceptions. In a league where some guys ride the bench before blossoming, then hang around too long, Riley was different. He hit the ground running and stopped when he was on top.

At right, Riley shows off the last of his three interceptions against Los Angeles. He had done three before, ruining Joe Namath's finale back in 1976.

In a display at his Florida home, Riley has all 65 INTs listed from his days as a master thief. There were the three picks against the Los Angeles Raiders' Jim Plunkett (Nos. 53-55) in 1982. But his three interceptions (Nos. 36-38) in a 42-3 victory over the New York Jets in the 1976 finale at Shea Stadium stand out. It was Hall of Famer Joe Namath's final game as a Jet. Riley picked Namath off twice and intercepted Richard Todd once.

"Guys get all excited about getting three interceptions in one game. I did it twice," Riley said. "I had (a club record) nine interceptions that year. Lemar (who had two picks) missed half the season and went to the Pro Bowl. I didn't even finish the Jets game because

Bill Waugh

42

I was having such a good game. Charley Winner was the DBs coach. He said, 'We don't want to get you hurt. We know you're in the Pro Bowl this year.' And he took me out. It happens like that."

Riley spent two years as a Green Bay assistant (1984-85) before returning to his alma mater. He served as FAMU's head coach from 1986-93, compiling a 48-39-2 record with two Mid-Eastern Athletic Conference titles and two MEAC Coach of the Year awards. He was the Black College Coach of the Year in 1988. He served as the school's athletic director from 1994 until January 2003. Riley was inducted into FAMU's Athletic Hall of Fame in 1977, but enshrinement in Canton eludes him.

"I think my numbers are deserving of the Hall of Fame," he said. "I've always been a modest and low-key type guy. I always thought your work would speak for you. It's like it's working against me now because the older you get and the longer you stay out of it, people forget who you are."

(Riley, 57, is semi-retired and living in his hometown of Bartow, Florida, where he serves on the Community Redevelopment Committee. His hobbies are hunting, fishing, and reading.)

The Scrambler

¶Virgil Carter, quarterback (1970-'73)

Before there was Joe Montana, there was Virgil Carter. An undersized guy with a modest arm, quick feet, and supreme intelligence, Carter bridged the gap between Greg Cook and Ken Anderson and was the Test Tube Baby for the West Coast Offense, which originated in Cincinnati under the direction of quarterbacks and receivers coach Bill Walsh.

College: Brigham Young
Hometown: Helendale, California
Height: 6-1,
Weight: 194

Walsh, a Bengals assistant from 1968-'75, perfected the offense as head coach of the San Francisco 49ers, winning three Super Bowls—two against Cincinnati—in a career that culminated in his induction into the Pro Football Hall of Fame in 1993.

"My memory of the Bill Walsh experience is realizing in advance of the world how good a coach he was and how gifted he was at designing plays," Carter said. "He credits me as the guy that he had to create the West Coast Offense for. His possession passes and quick decisions were all based on the offense we ran in 1970.

"He was able to take my abilities—which was the percentage pass and the ability to move and throw—and sculptured a successful offense around those abilities."

Carter was acquired in a trade with Buffalo to be Sam Wyche's backup in 1970 following Cook's career-ending shoulder injury in 1969. But Carter's arrival in Cincinnati likely wouldn't have occurred had it not been for a disagreement with Chicago Bears head coach Jim Dooley following the 1969 season.

Carter under the watchful eye of The Old Man, while (right), he scrambles for his life in a 27-31 loss to Cleveland on the lakefront in 1971.

44

A sixth-round draft pick of the Bears in 1967, Carter—buried on the depth chart behind Jack Concannon and Bobby Douglass—grumbled that he wasn't getting the playing time he deserved. "Like a lot of young, inexperienced quarterbacks, I complained because I didn't get the opportunity I thought was due," Carter said.

"I made a disparaging remark which was taken to heart by (Bears owner) George Halas, and I found myself being traded to Buffalo. There was very little opportunity or hope that I would complete a fourth year in the league. It was a strike season and during training camp we were late getting in. The Bills had drafted a guy named Dennis Shaw (a second-round

quarterback from San Diego State) and they thought he was going to be their future. So midway through a shortened training camp, I found myself in Cincinnati."

The Bengals were 1-6 in 1970 when Carter took over for a struggling Wyche and guided the team to seven straight victories, closing the regular season with an 8-6 record and winning the AFC Central Division in a "worst-to-first" climb to a championship in the club's third year of existence.

On November 15 that year, Carter became the only Bengals quarterback to rush for 100 yards in a game when he gained 110 on nine carries in a 14-10 victory over Cleveland in the first Bengals-Browns game at Riverfront Stadium. Carter unleashed a 73-yard

Bill Shepherd

Walt Kleine

47

Ryan Sanders

run in the game, but got hit from behind and fumbled the ball away.

"That whole march to the championship was important, but probably my proudest moment was returning to the Houston game (a 30-20 Bengals victory in December at the Astrodome) with 14 stitches in my tongue after having it almost lacerated off, finishing the game and winning so we had a chance to play for the playoff game the next week.

"Ron Pritchard gave me a forearm and basically severed my tongue within about a quarter of an inch and 14 stitches without anesthetic or pain pills were required at halftime.

"I played the second half and we engineered a victory. That, to me, summed up the spirit of that team and probably me as a quarterback—brittle yet gutsy.

"With the adrenalin in the game, it was OK, but when I got on the plane my tongue was swollen to the inside of my mouth. I couldn't even eat mashed potatoes. I had to drink the juice of boiled round steak for a week. I couldn't talk. Sam Wyche was calling the plays in practice while I was handing off and doing the maneuvers. I lost about 15 pounds that week."

The quarterback exposes one of his more vital parts—his tongue. After a Houston forearm in 1970, Carter needed a week on fluids and a teammate's voice to call signals.

Carter's gridiron efficiency may have originated in his bachelor's degree in physical and engineering science from BYU—he majored in statistics and minored in math. He also owns an MBA, with an emphasis in quantitative analysis, from Northwestern and taught statistics and math at Xavier University in the offseason.

One of his fondest memories is riding motorcycles and trail bikes with teammates Wyche, Bruce Coslet, Chip Myers, Ken Avery and Ken Dyer during the season. "We used to go out on Mondays, roast hotdogs, ride trail bikes and kind of kick back," Carter said. "That was a good group and a nucleus on that team as well."

What would've happened had Paul Brown found out about the motorcycle adventures?

"He might have known," Carter said, "but he wasn't paying us enough and we weren't known enough that it would've been much of a difference."

(Carter, 59, owns the Pi Omega Delta Insurance Services company in LaVerne, California, 25 miles east of Los Angeles. His firm writes doctor of chiropractic malpractice insurance. "Of the 10,000 chiropractors in the state, we insure about 1,300," he said. "Golf is my hobby, but a couple disintegrating discs in the lumbar region have caused me to back off.")

The Patriarch

¶Paul Brown, head coach (1968-'75)

The team plane had touched down at Greater Cincinnati/ Northern Kentucky Airport and, as was customary, head coach Paul Brown was making a beeline past the players' wives and girlfriends waiting at the terminal. Brown had taken great care in distancing himself from players and their families. But this day in 1970 was different. Linebacker Bill Bergey's wife, Micky, and the couple's infant son, Jason, were in the audience at the airport for the welcome home. "He saw my wife with this little baby in her arms," said Bergey, recounting his favorite story of P.B., "and he stopped. He kind of cupped the back of the baby's head and said, 'Mrs. Bergey, you made yourself a fine one right there.' All the wives and girlfriends just looked back. It was like, 'Oh, my God, he talked.' "

There is an endless litany of stories about Brown, the mastermind coach. He was, after all, the "Father of Pro Football," the great innovator who made the game a science and full-time business. He was the first to employ a year-round coaching staff; use notebooks, classroom and film study; and grade players from game film. He invented the face mask, and was the first to use intelligence tests as a clue to players' learning potential. He was first to call plays from the sideline by rotating guards as messengers, and he broke the major sport color barrier a year before Jackie Robinson entered Major League baseball.

Brown built the Cleveland Browns' dynasty with a career record of 167-53-8 from 1946-62, including four All-America Football Conference titles and three NFL crowns. He was enshrined in the Pro Football Hall of Fame in 1967, the same year he

PB (right), in a benevolent moment at the Wilmington College training camp in the Bengals' initial season, appeases fandom.

He changed the game forever. Whether they know it or not, nearly everyone in the game has been affected by Paul Brown.

—Pete Rozelle

Charles Steinbrunner

51

was awarded an American Football League franchise for the Queen City.

But the public saw only one side of him. The steely-eyed coach in the snap-brim hat, sport coat and tie staring grimly from the sidelines. Of course, there was another side to this coaching mountain, a softer side he kept hidden from fans.

Like the day cornerback Lemar Parrish entered the locker room before a game wearing a yellow and white jumpsuit, complete with long yellow coat and yellow wide-brimmed hat.

"Paul Brown came over and said, 'Let me try this on. Hey, I look pretty good in this,' " Parrish said. "The guys got quite a kick out of seeing Paul walk around with that on. He didn't usually do that kind of stuff."

What Brown did was rule the franchise with an iron fist, in what tight end Bob Trumpy called "a threatening manner. He'd say, 'If you don't listen to what I say, I'll ship your butt to Green Bay.' "

Brown was slight of build and so soft-spoken in meetings that sometimes players had to lean toward him just so they could hear him. But there was never any guessing on where he stood. Film sessions were particularly brutal.

"He'd walk in with his legal pad full of critiques and most of them weren't compliments," center Bob Johnson said. "He went person by person in front of the whole team, one position after the other. When he got to the offensive line, there were a bunch of sweaty palms and if he passed over you or if he didn't say anything terrible about you, you could breath a sigh of relief and lick your chops for what he was going to say about the running backs or whoever was next."

Brown was a control freak. Players who walked into meetings late got hit where it hurt most—the wallet. A hundred bucks a minute. He liked his players married, encouraged players to attend church on game-day Sunday mornings, and often preached that football was only one step toward a player's destiny in the real world. And he was a genius.

"At practice, in games, anywhere, he'd never raise his voice," said Dewey Warren, a backup quarterback on the inaugural '68 team. "He wanted you to listen. Maybe the play before messed up, and he'd say: 'Go back out and tell the right guard or the right tackle he better be blocking so and so.'

"He knew what everybody did on every play. And when the play broke down, he knew exactly where it happened and who made the mistake.

"In the short time I was around him, he absolutely amazed me for his knowledge. We'd practice an hour

> **I expect civilized table manners and table talk. There have been people who have failed to make this team simply because they were obnoxious to eat with.**
>
> —Paul Brown

Charlie Steinbrunner

53

and a half. He blew the whistle and that was it. Everything was so well organized. But he did say, 'Now if you feel like you need to do a little extra, you're men and I don't think I need to tell you.' Well, we wouldn't go in for another hour. You're scared to death to go off that field. You'd go over and throw, catch and do whatever. The DBs and linemen would work on stuff. Practice was over, but you wouldn't leave the field."

Dale Livingston, a punter and placekicker who lasted two seasons (1968-69), knew that feeling. He dropped back to punt, fumbled the ball, didn't get the punt off, and ran 12 yards for a first down. He came off the field and Brown said, "Don't you try that again." A few weeks later, Livingston tried it again, got thrown for a loss, and lay motionless on the field.

Trainer Marv Pollins went out to check on him. "What's wrong, Dale? Are you all right?" Pollins asked. "Yeah, I'm all right," Livingston said. "But don't take me off here. I don't want to see the Old Man yet."

The Old Man would give you "The Look." He'd raise and unfurl an eyebrow that meant you were in trouble. You could be wrong once, but you better not let it happen again.

John Murdough, the retired Bengals business manager, said old-time players would come to see Brown when the Bengals were on the road.

"In the Army, when you went in to see the commanding officer, you went to his desk, stood at attention and saluted," Murdough said. "These guys would come in to see Brown. They didn't salute, but they stood at attention. You could tell the respect they had for him."

Loathed by players who felt he ruled their lives, loved by players who welcomed the discipline, Brown could be as warm as a cozy fire or as chilly as a basement draft. Organized, professional, and fiercely loyal, he was a perfectionist who surrounded himself with great coaches.

"He definitely had some moments of fun, but fundamentally he was a solid leader with strong ideas and a strong personality," Johnson said. "The one thing you see with all successful coaches is they have a backbone that doesn't bend when push comes to shove. There is no vacillating when the team is at stake.

"Coach Brown was every bit a gentleman, but when you crossed the line, you crossed it and everybody knew it. He made it pretty obvious early on. If you're involved in a company and the boss fires somebody that needs to be fired, it says to everybody that marginal performance is not going to be tolerated. Coach Brown was very painfully honest."

I don't claim I brought anything to the game. I did my thing in my own style.

—Paul Brown

55

College:
Ohio State
Hometown:
Toledo, Ohio
Height: 6-5,
Weight:265

Chance Brockway

Textbook Tackle

¶Rufus Mayes, offensive tackle (1970-'78)

The late Rufus Mayes once said he didn't expect to go to L.A., emerge from an airplane, and get mobbed by fans. He understood that offensive linemen toil mostly in anonymity and don't rank high on the hero-worship scale. He also knew the offense couldn't function without the hogs in the trenches.

Mayes spent nine seasons in Cincinnati making a slew of running backs—Jess Phillips, Paul Robinson, Essex Johnson, Fred Willis, Doug Dressler, Boobie Clark, Charlie Davis, Lenvil Elliott, Stan Fritts, Archie Griffin, Pete Johnson, Deacon Turner, and Tony Davis—look good.

He also protected the blind side of quarterbacks Virgil Carter, Ken Anderson, John Reaves and, yes, even Dave Lewis. Although Mayes was never selected to the Pro Bowl, he was a human block of granite who used his quick feet, strong hands, broad shoulders, and long arms to keep defensive linemen from penetrating the backfield.

"He's like one of those guys if you'd go to a Sears catalogue and order an offensive tackle, that's what you'd get," center Bob Johnson said. "Was he a spectacular Anthony Munoz athlete? No. Was he great at any one thing? Probably not. But he was a good technician who was big enough and strong enough. He was a product of Ohio State—just a real good, solid, fundamental player."

Mayes, a Memphis, Tennessee, native who grew up in Toledo and starred at Macomber High School, always wanted to go to Ohio State, but his father nearly blew it for him on his recruiting visit. As dinner wound down at the swanky Jai Lai Restaurant in Columbus, head coach Woody Hayes took a spoon, leaned over, and asked Mayes' father if he could have a taste of his dessert.

"No, that's my dessert," said Rufus' dad, gobbling down his double fudge nut ball. Rufus was as stunned as Hayes at the rejection, but the coach never held it against the player, who became one of the school's most decorated linemen.

After an All-America senior year at Ohio State where he helped the 10-0

Mayes and his running mate at right tackle, Vern Holland, had only two losing seasons in the eight years they played together in Cincinnati.

Buckeyes to the 1968 National Championship and 27-16 Rose Bowl victory over O.J. Simpson's Southern Cal Trojans, Mayes was crowned the No. 1 draft pick (14th overall) of the Chicago Bears. He was immediately inserted as the starting right tackle and spent the season blocking for Hall of Fame tailback Gayle Sayers.

In order to get a player of Mayes' quality, the Bengals had to give up some quantity. So they traded defensive tackle Bill Staley and defensive end Harry Gunner to Chicago in exchange for Mayes in January 1970.

Cincinnati got the better end of that deal because Staley stayed two years with the Bears, while Gunner lasted only one. Paul Brown moved Mayes to left guard for a year, then he shared the left tackle job with Ernie Wright for a year before taking it over.

With bookend tackles Mayes on the left and Vernon Holland on the right, the Bengals finished at .500 or better in six of the eight years they played together. Pete Johnson, one of 18 Buckeyes to wear a Bengals uniform, idolized Mayes. "He was a born leader," Johnson said. "You could talk to him about anything. He never raised his voice and you never heard him say one bad word about anything—just straight up. And he was a great player. In pass blocking, he probably invented the use of the hands. Guys were not going to get around him. If he had been on a team like Dallas, he'd have been All-Pro every year."

Mayes wasn't one to trumpet himself. Wide receiver Isaac Curtis called Mayes "rangy with good feet and a very intelligent guy," but not always quiet. "He had this big booming laugh that echoed all over the place. But he was not one that ran his mouth all the time. He was quiet in a sense, but when Rufus started talking and laughing, you knew he was around."

Slowly, surely, Mayes saw left offensive tackle evolve into the skill position it is considered now. "Your recognition comes according to how your team plays," Mayes said in 1975. "If the team goes well, you'll get the recognition. It's even getting to where people recognize offensive linemen on the street."

Holland, known as "Suki," went to an autograph session one night and got paid a compliment—sort of. Fans called him "Rufus." Ahh, the price of fame.

(Mayes died on January 9, 1990, of bacterial meningitis in Seattle. He was 42. Upon retirement from the NFL in 1979, he became a marketing representative for Hewlett-Packard Company, in Bellevue, Washington. He lived in Redmond, Washington, with his wife and son.)

Chance Brockway

The Game-breaker

¶Lemar Parrish, cornerback (1970-'77)

Bengals fans know him as "Leapin' Lemar," but his close friends call him, simply, "Leap." And nobody leaped higher than Lemar Parrish. He graced the Bengals secondary and special teams for eight seasons and left a legacy as the most aggressive, explosive, competitive and exciting defensive back in club history. His accomplishments are staggering, starting with his club-record 13 touchdowns "by return and recovery"—four interception returns, four punt returns, three fumble returns, one kickoff return, and one blocked field goal return—and his incredible 18.8-yard, punt-return average (18 for 338 yards) in 1974.

College: Lincoln University
Hometown: Riviera Beach, Florida
Height: 5-11, Weight: 185
Pro Bowls: 6

"I was a game-breaker," Parrish said. "My stats will attest to that. For being a seventh-round draft pick, they got their money's worth. In fact, they got more than their money's worth."

Parrish is the only player in club history to score two TDs in a game under the special "return and recovery" category, and he did it three times. He had a 95-yard kickoff return and an 83-yard return of a blocked field goal at Buffalo on November 8, 1970. He had interception returns of 25 and 33 yards at Houston on December 17, 1972. And he had a 90-yard punt return and a 47-yard fumble return against Washington on October 6, 1974.

With Parrish at left corner and partner-in-crime Ken "The Rattler" Riley—who piled up 65 career interceptions—at right corner, the duo terrorized NFL quarterbacks from sea to shining sea.

"Riley and I complemented each other," Parrish said. "I was really more aggressive. I was a gambler. If the ball's in the air, I'm going for it. Riley would do the same thing. He was a helluva cornerback. My thing was, once I'd pick it off, I was gone. I had such

Parrish's speed amazed even his position coach, and no less an authority than Paul Brown said, "He accelerates faster than any player I've ever coached."

Skip Peterson

Wally Nelson

63

tight coverage, they wouldn't throw there much. I made the Pro Bowl several times with just two or three interceptions because of the respect they had for me. That was the difference."

In Parrish's mind, 12 of his TDs are a blur. But one stands out. It was the 95-yard kickoff return at Buffalo. "I had come close many times and never busted. I always got tripped up," he said. "But Paul Brown told the press before the game: 'It's time for Lemar Parrish to break one. He's right there.' We played Buffalo, and I broke one. I always ran to daylight, you understand? I knew where my wall was supposed to be, but I'd take the first break I could get. I ran off instinct. All your great ones do that."

Sundays were easy for Parrish because practices were so difficult. After all, he was matched against teammates Isaac Curtis, Charlie Joiner, Speedy Thomas, and Chip Myers in practice. "To me, they were the best in the league," he said.

Parrish's departure after the '77 season has long been a sore point with management. He wanted money the club wasn't willing to pay. So they dealt him to Washington, where he earned two more trips to the Pro Bowl (1979-'80) in a four-year stint with the Redskins before closing out his 13-year career with Buffalo in 1982.

"I loved the Bengals organization and the players," Parrish said. "That was like family to me. I never wanted to be traded. But I had contract problems and I just couldn't get the money that I was worth. I didn't want to go, but it was business. It was more than just a game because I realized I couldn't play this game all my life and I need to make the money while I was on top."

Following his retirement, Parrish's life spiraled downhill when he got involved in drugs. But he checked himself into a treatment center in Chattanooga, Tennessee, in 1986, and got himself together. He returned to Lincoln University, secured his bachelor's degree with a major in physical education and a minor in psychology, and is working toward another degree in special education.

"I didn't know why I had to do certain things," he said. "I realized I needed professional help. I went to treatment and was serious about it. It completely turned my life around. I've been down that path of destruction and I am not looking back at it."

(Parrish, 57, is the defensive coordinator for Lincoln University, an NCAA Division II school in Jefferson City, Missouri. He previously served as the Blue Tigers' defensive backs coach, but got promoted following the 2002 season. Shooting pool and swimming are his hobbies.)

Wally Nelson

Piano Man

Mike Reid, defensive tackle (1970-'74)

Teammates had seen Mike Reid angry before, but nothing like this. When he reached the sideline, he was in full-blown cursing and screaming mode—with good reason. He had just sustained a fractured pinkie, and it meant he couldn't play the piano for two months. A musician without his instrument? Now *that's* torture. "All I remember is him coming off the field and just ranting and raving, and blaming everybody for his broken finger," linebacker Jim LeClair said. "He was just outrageously upset, about as angry as any individual could get. It was a great moment."

College: Penn State
Hometown: Altoona, Pennsylvania
Height: 6-4,
Weight: 258
Pro Bowls: 2

A moment that speaks volumes about Reid. On the field, he was a Tyrannosaurus Rex, overpowering offensive linemen, devouring quarterbacks, and engulfing ball carriers. But caressing the keyboard of his piano soothed the savage beast in him, and after five seasons of football brilliance, he turned to the love of his life—music—full-time.

Today he is a Nashville-based Grammy-winning songwriter, penning hits for Willie Nelson ("There You Are"), Ronnie Milsap ("Stranger in My House"), Kenny Rogers, Bette Midler, Wynonna Judd, and Bonnie Raitt, whose rendition of "I Can't Make You Love Me" sold over 6 million copies.

But in the NFL of the early 1970s, he was the pride of Penn State, earning NFL Defensive Rookie of the Year and reaching the Pro Bowl twice by playing football with the abandon of a hungry Nittany Lion.

"He had tremendous quickness off the ball," quarterback Virgil Carter said. "But he didn't have a football temperament. That's what was so surprising. The artist playing football was a dichotomy in personalities."

Reid may have stunned the football world by walking away from the game, but his teammates couldn't have been too surprised. They had to have seen it coming. He often tested his musical talent on guest appearances with the Cincinnati Pops and other orchestras, and he tolerated football more than he treasured it.

To fight the boredom at training During July scrimmages at training camp, the other players kidded The Piano Man about his avocation. "His hands!" they yelled when the ball was snapped. "Get his hands!"

I would almost say he didn't like football. He didn't like to practice at all. For his position, he wasn't very big. He was just incredibly quick.

—Bob Trumpy

Walt Kleine

"Mike was an absolutely magnificent football player. He was quick as a cat and strong as a bull.

—Tommy Casanova

69

camp, Bob Johnson, Bob Trumpy, and Bruce Coslet would drag Reid into a room with a piano at Wilmington College. "We'd say, 'You're going to entertain us,'" Johnson said. "He'd say, 'Ah, crap, I don't want to do this.' We'd sit him down and physically hold him there until he played a little bit. Finally, he'd get going. We'd wander off after 20 or 25 minutes and he'd be there for three hours. We'd have to drag him back for bed check."

Former Bengals business manager John Murdough fondly recalled one assignment he lined up for Reid. "The Delta Queen was coming into Cincinnati," Murdough said, "and I got Mike to come down early in the morning and play the calliope.

"We got on as soon as it docked and he started playing. There was a big crowd down on the landing. It was one of those cold spring mornings and he told me, 'Don't do me any more favors.' His hands were cold up there playing the calliope, but they gave him such applause that he kept on playing."

The best story is from his roommate, Tommy Casanova. The Bengals escaped Cincinnati in the autumn of 1973 for a game in San Diego. "Back in Cincinnati, it was overcast and dreary," said Casanova. "In San Diego, it was 80 degrees and beautiful. We stayed at a U-shaped hotel on the beach. I woke up at 5 o'clock and walked out on the balcony 15 floors up.

"Dawn was cracking, the sun was rising, and I went back in and told Mike, who was lying in bed, 'Mike, come out and see what a beautiful morning this is.' So he walks out on the balcony with just a towel on. There's about a half-dozen guys down at a table around the pool drinking Bloody Marys. And he starts bellowing out, 'Oh, What a Beautiful Mornin'.'

"He's singing and it's reverberating inside this U-shaped place—just *echoing*. And people are stumbling out on their balcony half-dressed trying to figure out what the hell's going on. He completes the song, I'm

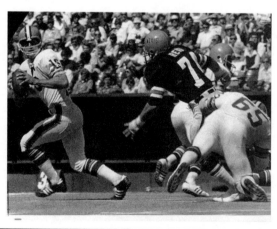

Jim Rutledge

70

hiding back in the room because I'm embarrassed, and he gets a standing ovation from these drunks down by the pool. He didn't care."

Reid, the big ham, was blessed with a gift for communicating with his audience. He was all hard knocks on the road to gridiron glory, but all heart away from the football frenzy.

(Reid, 57, quit the NFL in 1975 to play keyboards for the Apple Butter Band in Cincinnati. In 1980, he moved to Nashville, befriended Ronnie Milsap, and the rest is history. "It was another life," Reid told Cincinnati icon Nick Clooney, about his football career.)

71

Tiny Augustana

¶Ken Anderson, quarterback (1971-'86)

For his 55th birthday, Ken Anderson's wife, Cristy, gave him a present he'll forever treasure—the 1970 through 1975 Bengals highlights from NFL Films on DVD. He's grateful for the gift because the flood of memories it provides is like nectar from the football gods. "You know what surprised me?" he said. "How good we were. We were real good. Unfortunately, we were a tad overshadowed by the Steelers. But, gosh, we were good, and our defense was so good. I had forgotten about that."

College: Augustana
Hometown: Batavia, Illinois
Height: 6-3,
Weight: 212
Pro Bowls: 4

Anderson had forgotten because he was too busy writing the Bengals' record book during his 16-year career —a franchise record for service. Let's divulge his statistics before we dig into his head, OK?

He's the Bengals' career leader in pass completions (2,654), passing yards (32,838), and touchdown passes (197). He owns the NFL record for highest completion percentage in a season with a blistering 70.55 in 1982, eclipsing the old mark of 70.3 set by Sammy Baugh in 1945. He won four NFL passing titles, was named to four Pro Bowls, led the league three times in lowest interception percentage, and twice has been among 15 finalists for election to the Pro Football Hall of Fame.

Not too shabby for an Illinois prep legend who arrived as a third-round draft pick in 1971 from NCAA Division III Augustana College in Rock Island, Illinois.

"Had Greg Cook not gotten hurt (as a rookie in '69), I never would have been a Cincinnati Bengal," Anderson said. "Greg was a great talent and had that unfortunate shoulder injury. When they drafted me, Greg would have been in his third

A mathematics major in college, Anderson showed measured consistency as quarterback, a highly efficient player in a highly efficient system.

He likes
his family,
likes to
play his
game, and
likes to
drink beer.
He should
have been
a hockey
player.

—Bob
Trumpy

Ty Greenlees (left) and Charles Steinbrunner

73

year. My gosh, he led the AFC in passing as a rookie, so there's no need for me. But it was nice for me to come into a young team that had experienced some success. It was great to start off my career playing for a guy like Paul Brown, and playing for a coach like Bill Walsh, to give me a good solid foundation. There were a lot of good things for me."

Anderson was accused of being a robotic player. That's because his throwing motion was pure, his release point consistent, and his accuracy laser-like. Here's a guy who completed 20 straight passes in a 35-27 victory over the Houston Oilers in the Astrodome in the 1982 regular-season finale.

Mike Brown called Anderson "the most important player in the history of our franchise." But many think his no-frills Midwestern demeanor has helped keep him out of Canton.

"I was efficient, accurate, could execute the game plan the way the coaches wanted it, and could carry the offense if I had to. The term 'robotic' comes because for all those years Paul Brown, Bill Walsh, and Lindy Infante called the plays. I was in a very effective system and that's the way Paul Brown had always operated."

Anderson's best statistical game was a 33-24 victory over Buffalo on November 17, 1975—the first Monday night game in Cincinnati —when he exploded for 447 passing yards and two TDs.

"But you've got to go back to the AFC Championship game (Freezer Bowl) for the most memorable,"

I'd take him over Terry Bradshaw in a heartbeat. He was more accurate. You want a QB that won't lose a game for you. Well, Anderson didn't lose many games.

—Bob Johnson

Charles Steinbrunner (left) and Chance Brockway

75

he said. "What was at stake in that game, the conditions we played in, and how well we played as a team. That's got to be the highlight of it."

Anderson conquered his share of adversity, too. In August of 1978, he suffered a broken right hand while striking a Green Bay pass-rusher as he released the ball in the third quarter of the final preseason game.

Out for six to eight weeks, he volunteered to play after the Bengals lost their first four games. The action was noble but premature. He threw four interceptions in a 28-12 loss at San Francisco, and head coach Bill "Tiger" Johnson was replaced by Homer Rice the next day.

Bengals fans will also never forget the opening game of the 1981 Super Bowl season against Seattle at Riverfront Stadium. Anderson was intercepted three times and the Bengals fell behind, 21-0. Head coach Forrest Gregg benched Anderson and inserted third stringer Turk Schonert —Jack Thompson was out with a bruised knee—as the Bengals roared back to win, 27-21.

Gregg initially said Thompson or Schonert would start the next week against the New York Jets, but he reconsidered and stuck with Anderson, who passed for 246 yards and two TDs in a 31-30 victory at Shea Stadium—and the rest is history.

Anderson ended up throwing for 3,754 yards and 29 touchdowns in winning the NFL passing title and leading the Bengals into Super Bowl XVI. He was also voted the 1981 NFL Player of the Year.

"Forrest was exactly what we needed at that point in our history," Anderson said. "He was a tough, demanding coach. He's what we needed to come in and turn the thing around. And he did it in two years.

"I was very fortunate to play with a bunch of good players who were even better people. There are so many guys I love and respect. There are guys you may not see for five years, but I could call if I needed them today and they'd be here."

Anderson's 32-year affiliation with the Bengals as a player, broadcaster, and assistant coach ended on December 30, 2002, when team president Mike Brown began pursuit of a new coaching staff in the wake of Dick LeBeau's firing.

(Anderson, 55, is in his second season as an assistant coach for the NFL Jacksonville Jaguars. After coaching the QBs in 2003, he's now in charge of the wide receivers. "My hobby is golf—as much as I can stand," he said.)

Anderson vs. the Dallas Cowboys in December of 1985, engineering a 50-24 win at Riverfront Stadium.

Anderson was always in great condition. We'd run before the season and there'd be seven or eight of us out there and he'd always talk us into running these 120-yard strides that were damn-near full speed. He'd end up leaving everybody panting.

—Bob Johnson

Matinee Idol

¶ Tommy Casanova, strong safety (1972-'77)

He ran like the wind, hit like a truck, and covered like a blanket. So why did he do it? Why did Tommy Casanova walk away from the game he loved at the peak of his career with the Bengals? As the legendary Vince Lombardi said: "The knee. Always the knee." Only in Casanova's case, it was *both* knees.

College:
Louisiana
State
Hometown:
Crowley,
Louisiana
Height: 6-2,
Weight: 200
Pro Bowl: 3

The handsome dude with the ball-hawking skills, who had a wide receiver's speed and a linebacker's mentality, who made women weak in the knees with his easy smile and rugged good looks, retired after six seasons at age 27 because he simply had more than enough of the pounding and wanted to finish medical school.

"My knees had just worn out," said Casanova, one of the best safeties in club history. "I'd limp all week and play on Sundays, then limp all week again. I wasn't thinking about Pittsburgh or Cleveland. I was thinking about my knees.

"It got to the point where I didn't feel like I was able to do for the team what I needed to do, and I didn't want to play just for the sake of money. I wanted to play because I loved the game, and when I felt like I wasn't playing at my maximum, it was time to retire. I had a year of medical school left and it was time to devote my attention to medicine. It was a tough decision, but it was time. Football just wasn't fun anymore."

At least not like it used to be. It was fun getting voted to three Pro Bowls and posing for pictures with teammates Coy Bacon, Jim LeClair, Lemar Parrish, and Isaac

Casanova was a great college player who had sprinter's speed and uncommon reactions, his flair carrying into the pros where he was sensational even as a rookie.

Curtis in Hawaii. It was fun snaring 17 career interceptions and scoring four touchdowns—two interceptions, one punt return and one fumble return.

And it was fun rooming with the unpredictable Piano Man, Mike Reid, on the road. Reid would play the piano and sing, and have teammates bending over with laughter from his stand-up comedy routines.

A second-round draft pick from LSU, Casanova's name is splattered throughout the Bengals' record book. His two interceptions for TDs came in 1976 and his 17 thefts rank fifth in club history.

He also has the third most punt returns (91) in club annals, and his 8.6 yards per punt return is fourth best in team history.

"I was blessed with pretty good speed for a safety and that allowed me to be fairly successful," he said.

"But my biggest asset was Chuck Weber, the defensive backfield coach. He really taught me man-to-man technique and positioning. Chuck went through the ordeal of stripping me down and changing me over and giving me a new perspective on coverage."

Casanova attended the University of Cincinnati medical school in the summers during his NFL career. Medicine was the magnet that finally pulled him off the field. It was much easier on his knees. That's why he has empathy for any young NFL player who retires early because of injuries.

79

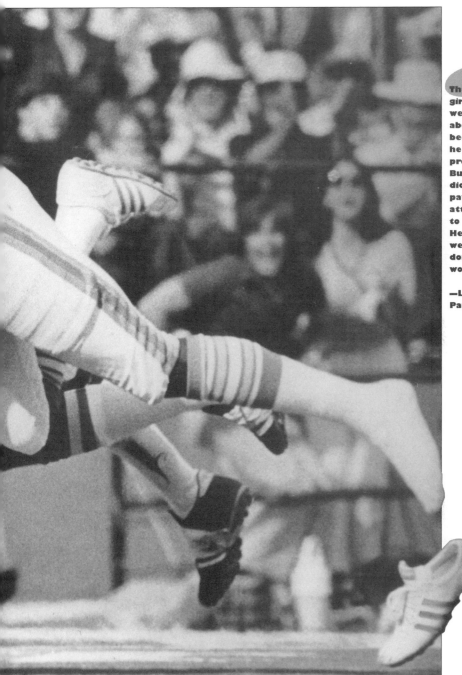

"The girls were crazy about him because he was a pretty boy. But he didn't pay no attention to 'em. He just went about doing his work.

—Lemar Parrish

"It's always wise to walk away while you're still walking, and football is not the end of your life," Casanova said. "It's an opportunity for a lot of young men to take advantage of early in their lives. But by no means is that the end of it."

Casanova has no regrets about his early exit. He claims he doesn't remember the wins and losses, that they all just blend together, forming one lasting beautiful memory.

But every once in a while he'll awaken to a faster heartbeat and remember the blood, sweat and cheers on the Sundays of yesteryear.

"If there's anything I hope people associate with me is that I played 60 minutes as hard as I could," Casanova said. "I hope fans remember that I was a team player, and I never quit."

(Casanova, 54, is an ophthalmologist in Crowley, Louisiana. "I do a lot of cataract surgery and eyelid reconstructive-type surgery," he said. His hobbies are hunting, fishing and coaching Pee-Wee basketball. He also owns a farm outside Cincinnati in Adams County, where he hunts turkey and deer.)

The fearless Casanova scuffles with Pittsburgh receiver Theo Bell in a difficult 7-3 loss in late November of 1976 at Riverfront Stadium. It was, however, the only home loss of the season.

Bill Garlow

True Grit

¶Jim LeClair, linebacker(1972-'83)

When Bengals fans close their eyes, they can still see Jim LeClair coming to the ropes and signing autographs during those long, grueling training camps in the sweltering heat at Wilmington College. "You remember that bushy hair and those sideburns? Well, they're all gone," LeClair said. "Now I fight to keep hair." Speaking of coming to the ropes and of fighting, who could forget that summer day in 1975 when LeClair fought Victor the Wrestling Bear to a draw at the Cincinnati Convention Center?

College: North Dakota Hometown: South St. Paul, Minnesota Height: 6-3, Weight:234 Pro Bowl:1

LeClair spent his first six seasons in Cincinnati as a member of the U.S. Army Reserves. As part of his two weeks of active duty prior to training camp in the summer of 1975, LeClair landed at a display booth at the "Sport, Boat and Travel Show" downtown, doing promotional work for the Reserves.

"I was working at the Convention Center the whole week and every day they had this wrestling bear that would just take guys and throw 'em down and just manhandle them," LeClair said. "Every day I'm there, these guys from the Reserves are on me, saying, 'You wrestled in college, you should go out and wrestle the bear and see if you can do anything.' That's the last thing I wanted to do. I might get hurt.

"By the time the end of the week came, I was being coaxed about four or five times a day to wrestle the bear. So I said, 'OK, I'll wrestle the bear.' "

The event was advertised and anywhere from 400 to 500 people, including teammates, packed an arena inside the Convention Center to see the Bengals middle linebacker take on the 6-foot-5, 476-pound black bear.

Victor had on a muzzle, was de-clawed and de-fanged. But he had a real long tongue that kept licking LeClair's face—and Victor's breath smelled like a garbage dump.

"So I start wrestling this bear," LeClair said. "I watched him all week and he was leaning on these people. He'd have all his weight on them, they'd get wobbly-legged, and he'd throw 'em down and pin 'em. He was going through contestants like you wouldn't believe.

LeClair had size, quick reactions, and a philosophy of aggression. "It's better you knock the other guy down," he said, "than he knocks you down."

6 Once, I went downfield and cut him with a borderline cheap shot. I didn't know it was him. About five plays later, I'm running down the field and he gave me one of those Dick Butkus clotheslines under the chin. 'Now we're even,' he said. 'Jimmy,' I said, 'I didn't know it was you!'

—Dan Ross

I enjoyed
the physical
aspect
of the
game.

—Jim
LeClair

Walt Kleine

87

"I said, 'I can't let him do that to me,' so I kept taking his paws or arms and putting them under my arms instead of on my shoulders, so he couldn't lean on me. That kind of threw the bear off. He was kind of pulling back from me and I grabbed his leg and pulled it up from underneath him and he went right on his back. Then I jumped on top of him. The bear pushed me up with his paws and tried to spin me off him. I caught myself just in time to not get knocked off .

"As it turned out, the bear-keeper basically

declared it a tie, because I couldn't roll him up on his shoulders to pin him. I was trying to move 400 pounds of butt. Nonetheless, he said it was a tie. But when the people ask me, I always say, 'I let the bear up, he didn't let me up.' So that's what happened. Now you've got the inside scoop."

LeClair, of course, didn't have to fight to keep his reputation as one of the toughest, grittiest, and best middle linebackers in Bengals history. A third-round draft pick from the University of North Dakota in 1972, LeClair was a role player who excelled in special teams coverage his first two

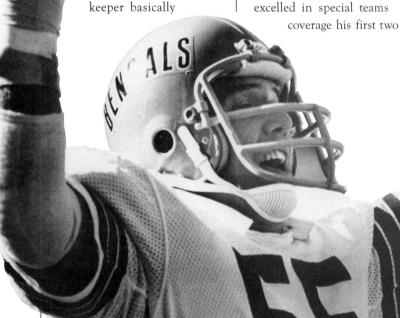

Walt Kleine

88

years, then broke into the starting lineup in 1974 after head coach Paul Brown traded Bill Bergey to Philadelphia. LeClair earned Pro Bowl honors in 1976.

"It was a real encouragement to myself to see that they had the confidence that I was able to do the job," LeClair said. "And that's really all I needed. From there it was history. You're trying to prove yourself as a player and all these different thoughts run through your mind and to have that type of a psychological boost, having them show that type of confidence in me was really a plus for myself.

"As a player I felt it was my role to be the leader on the defense and do two things—be a leader from the standpoint of how I played the game and also be a leader from the standpoint of encouragement to my fellow teammates. That's what I felt my obligation and responsibility was."

LeClair recalled the disappointment of Super Bowl XVI and the San Francisco 49ers' goal-line stand at the 1:17 mark of the third quarter with the Bengals trailing 20-7.

LeClair had three straight seasons of 100-plus tackles, a mark that wasn't broken until Takeo Spikes did it in 2001. He held the team tackling title four times, topped only by Tim Krumrie's five titles.

"What was most discouraging was our inability to get in the end zone from the one-foot line," he said. "That was probably the most memorable moment—the disappointment that we didn't score. When they hold you on the goal line in the Super Bowl, it's a pretty uplifting thing from their standpoint. They gained momentum and we lost points. It's not a good situation to be in.

"I don't dwell on that game that much—not anymore. For the first couple of years, I thought about it quite a bit, but other than that, no. Time kind of heals all wounds. It's been long enough that I'm over it.

"If there's a legacy that I left it was maybe just the guy that came to play all the time. I enjoyed the physical aspect of the game, the competition of the game, and the strategy of the game. I was always ready to play, I enjoyed the game. I had fun at the games. When you can say that and look back on a career that I had, it's really a credit."

(LeClair, 54, is mayor of Mayville, N.D., a community of 2,000 located between Grand Forks and Fargo on the eastern edge of North Dakota. He sold one business—Evergreen Marketing Management Ltd., an agriculture production company—and works at his insurance business, LeClair & Associates. Racquetball and woodworking are his hobbies.)

> "We're in a goal-line play and Jimmy was standing like a rock with waves crashing against him, screaming at the top of his lungs, the veins popping on his neck. I remember saying, 'So that's how you play goal-line defense.'
>
> —Reggie Williams

The Ice Man

¶Isaac Curtis, wide receiver (1973-'84)

He was a smooth route-runner with graceful, flowing strides, possessed world-class speed and great hands. Was that glue on his fingertips? No. It only seemed that way. And when the Bengals needed a big reception, there was no question who they'd turn to—Isaac Curtis. "The Ice Man," teammate Pete Johnson said. "That's what we called him. He was just like a gazelle running down the field. If the ball was anywhere within reach, he was going to grab it. He had probably the most fantastic one-hand catches you'd ever want to see. You could do a highlight film on him."

College: San Diego State
Hometown: Santa Ana, California
Height: 6-1,
Weight: 192
Pro Bowl: 4

Coming out of San Diego State in 1973 after playing one season for legendary coach Don "Air" Coryell, Curtis was the apple of Cleveland owner Art Modell's eye. The Browns wanted him with the 16th overall pick, but the Bengals— drafting 15th— "one-upped" their Ohio rival and stole him away. The Browns got popular Arizona State wideout Steve Holden, who lasted four seasons (1973-'76) in Cleveland. But the Bengals got a four-time

Pro Bowler who remains the club leader in receiving yards.

Not once in Curtis' glorious career did he achieve a 1,000-yard season, but he always seemed to come through in the clutch. He caught 416 passes for 7,101 yards—a franchise-record 17.1 yards per catch—and 53 TDs.

"Every indication I had was that the Browns were going to pick me," Curtis said. "I had no idea the Bengals had any interest in me. I'd seen 'em around at our games, but they never talked to me."

Curtis was recruited by San Diego State in high school, but the Aztecs— members of The Big West Conference—didn't have a freshman

In an October, 1977, session at Spinney Field, the Ice Man exhibits the customary nonchalance he demonstrated in both practice and game.

90

If I could get man to man, I didn't think there was anybody in the league that could run with me.

—Isaac Curtis

Skip Peterson

91

football program at the time. He had no interest in attending junior college, so he enrolled at Cal-Berkeley where he spent three years starring on the track team, but wasting away as a little-used running back. Cal's athletic department went on probation after Curtis' junior year. Athletes were allowed to transfer without losing eligibility as long as they transferred out of the Pacific 8 Conference.

For "Ike," who was clocked at 9.3 seconds in the 100-yard dash on Cal's championship track team, it was an easy choice. "Air" Coryell took to the skies with the high-flying Curtis. "I wasn't real happy at Cal being a running back," Curtis said. "I thought I should be playing wide receiver. I asked if I could be moved, but they wanted me at running back and I wasn't running very much. I couldn't figure that out. Here I was a world-class sprinter, and I was doing more blocking than anything. I had the best hands on the team. I needed to be someplace where I could be more effective.

"Looking back, transferring to San

"Riverfront Stadium. Kenny Anderson. Hits his main man. Right there. No. 85. And Eye-Sac Curtis. Goes. All. The. Way."— Howard Cosell, Monday Night Football.

Diego State was the best thing that probably ever happened to me because they made a receiver out of me."

Curtis spent his pro career tormenting the Browns, starting in '73 when he caught three TD passes—covering nine, 70, and 20 yards—in the first half, igniting the Bengals' 34-17 victory in Cincinnati on December 9. Curtis and quarterback Ken Anderson clicked that day, and Browns cornerbacks Ben Davis, Clarence Scott, and Clifford Brooks were helpless trying to stop them.

"We were always able to get myself isolated on whoever I wanted," Curtis said. "They played a lot of man-to-man. They gave me a lot of room because of my speed. Kenny and myself, we were pretty confident that if I could get man to man, I didn't think there was anybody in the league that could run with me. So the advantage was with us."

Curtis called it his most memorable game. The Bengals won the final six regular-season games that year to finish 10-4, capture the AFC Central Division, and qualify for the playoffs.

"I can remember Paul Brown coming up to me and, of course, being a rookie, he didn't say a whole lot to me that year. But he came up and kind of grabbed me by the arm and said, 'That was something special.' It was a pretty memorable moment for a rookie."

(*Curtis, 54, is national sales director for Winegardner & Hammons Inc., a hotel management company based in the Cincinnati suburb of Blue Ash. His No. 1 hobby is golf, but he also hunts.*)

"Isaac owned the Browns. He was good for two TDs a game against them.

—Ken Anderson

Bill Waugh (left) and Skip Peterson

93

The Tool

¶Dave Lapham, offensive line (1974-'83)

On the clock in the third round of the 1974 draft, with the 61st overall pick at stake, the Bengals figured it was "Tool Time." So they grabbed a tough, feisty, rangy offensive tackle from Syracuse who became one of the most beloved linemen in club history. Dave Lapham, who had already been drafted by Birmingham of the World Football League, remembers it like it was yesterday.

College: Syracuse
Hometown: Wakefield, Massachusetts
Height: 6-4,
Weight: 262

"There was no ESPN or anything like that," he recalled. "You're just sitting by the phone. It's 6 o'clock at night. I thought the draft was over. It was 17 rounds then. I get a call from the Cleveland Browns and they said, 'Have you signed with the WFL yet?' I said, 'No, I haven't signed. I want to play in the NFL.' They said, 'OK, that's all we wanted to know. Stay by your phone.'

"The phone rings two minutes later and I'm thinking it's Cleveland. I answered the phone and said, 'Cleveland?' Pete Brown's secretary in player personnel said, 'No, no, this is the Cincinnati Bengals. You better not ever say *that* word again.' Then she said, 'Here, your offensive line coach, Bill Johnson, wants to speak with you.' And he says, 'Yeah, never say that team, Cleveland Browns, again.' I'm like, oh, *geez*, my first taste of the rivalry."

Lapham was a passionate team player but what separated him from other linemen was his versatility. Teammates nicknamed him "The Tool" because he was used everywhere on the offensive line. Listed in the club's media guide as a center, guard, and tackle, he played all five line positions in the same game twice in his 10-year career.

Why?

Because he could.

"That was something I just decided I wanted to try," he said. "I'd get graded on not just my assignments every play, but everybody else's. If I was pulling, was the center reaching? Was the tackle blocking down? Was the fullback filling? I just wanted to know what everybody around me was doing. I was getting the big picture. That really helped me.

"Paul Brown and Tiger Johnson encouraged that—just understanding

At right, Lapham blocks for Ken Anderson, en route to a 447-yard passing night vs. Buffalo—and the divisional playoffs—in 1975.

as much as you could about defensive configurations, schemes, what they were trying to do, and then offensively how it was being attacked."

Lapham's most memorable moments stem from the 1981 season when a 27-7 victory over San Diego in the AFC championship game—the Freezer Bowl—spilled over into Super Bowl XVI, a 26-21 loss to San Francisco at the Pontiac Silverdome.

Riverfront Stadium was in a deep freeze for the AFC title game on January 10, 1982. It was minus-9 degrees with a wind-chill factor of minus-59 degrees—the second-coldest game in NFL history behind Green Bay's 21-17 win over Dallas at Lambeau Field on December 31, 1967.

"I remember going out there sleeveless and seeing the looks on the Chargers' faces," Lapham said.

"They were looking at us like we were crazy, which we were. It was a psychological advantage and also it was an advantage because their defensive linemen were great pass rushers. I was playing against Gary "Big Hands" Johnson. He was a grabber and I just didn't want to have cloth on my arms for him to grab. They did allow us to put Vaseline on our exposed skin. I just put Vaseline on there and it worked well."

So did the Bengals, who dominated the game from the beginning. "Winning the AFC championship game was an incredible moment," Lapham said. "Going into that locker room and the looks on everybody's faces. That's the cornball stuff, but that's what you play the game for, really.

"The Super Bowl, obviously, is

memorable. But it's not as good a memory, whereas the Freezer Bowl is famous because of all the circumstances around it and because we won the game. The difficult environment, the adversity that we had to overcome to win the game is the reason that it's the most memorable."

Lapham visited the Silverdome many times as a Bengals broadcaster since Super Bowl XVI. Each time, he would stand in the press box looking down at the end zone, paralyzed by the memory of the 49ers' goal-line stand.

"The reason the Super Bowl is memorable to me is it's the best and worst I've felt in the same day professionally in my life," he said. "I remember how excited and ready we were, and all the anticipation before the game, and then how awful it felt later. You talk about the very, very top, the peak of the roller coaster, down to the very, very bottom in a four-hour time frame. It was amazing."

(Lapham, 52, enters his 19th season as the analyst on Bengals radio broadcasts. The games are aired on Clear Channel flagship radio stations WCKY-AM (1360), WOFX-FM (92.5) and WLW-AM (700). He is also a football analyst on TV, working the Big 12 Conference game of the week for FOX Sports Net, plus the Cotton Bowl, NFL games and NFL Europe League games for FOX. Lapham is a passionate basketball, baseball, and hockey fan, plus a highly-visible public speaker year-round in the Cincinnati area. "Most of my hobbies are sports related," he said. "I'm a sports junkie.")

Chance Brockway

Sack Man

¶Coy Bacon, defensive end (1976-'77)

College:
Jackson
State
Hometown:
Ironton,
Ohio
Height: 6-4,
Weight: 280
Pro Bowl: 2

From the halls of Ironton High School to the shores of Riverfront Stadium, Coy Bacon returned to his home state when he joined the Bengals in 1976. His flame burned brightly for two seasons in Cincinnati and then, sadly, it flickered out and he was gone again, off to another team. But it sure was fun while it lasted. NFL historians refer to Bacon as a journeyman defensive end because he played for four teams in a 14-year span—the Los Angeles Rams (1968-'72), San Diego Chargers (1973-'75), Bengals and Washington Redskins (1978-'81). But he'll tell you—and so will his teammates, his enemies, and his statistics—that he was the most devastating pass rusher in Cincinnati history.

The league didn't start recording individual quarterback sacks until 1982—the season after he retired. But the Bengals' records show he generated a single-season, club-record 22 sacks in 1976 when the team went 10-4, only to miss the playoffs.

That's an incomprehensible total in today's game, especially considering the last Bengal with double-digit sacks was Alfred Williams with 10 in 1992. But Coy said he actually brought home more bacon than that.

"The Bengals don't recognize all my sacks, either," he said. "I know they've got me for 22. But on film, it's 26."

With a mastodon's size, coupled with a monstrous appetite for devouring quarterbacks, Bacon could bull-rush left offensive tackles from his right end position, but often didn't because that tactic wasn't necessary. As strong as he was, his quickness, balance, and technique were even better.

He'd smack tackles hard enough to shock them, feel their weight, pick the proper side, and rumble past them to the quarterback.

"I always thought that when Coy Bacon got on AstroTurf, he was about as good a pass rusher as there was," Cleveland Browns venerable left tackle Doug Dieken said. "He was a different player up at our place on the grass field, but he drove me nuts."

Center Bob Johnson called Coy Bacon the best pass rusher the Bengals ever had, as well as probably the best defensive lineman.

My style was a lot of movement off the ball.

—Coy Bacon

Chance Brockway

99

"I personally think he's the best pass rusher that the Bengals have ever had and probably the best defensive lineman," Bengals center Bob Johnson added. "He was big and strong. He was 280 when people weren't that big."

Bacon learned his technique playing basketball in high school. He'd explode off the line of scrimmage, swinging those big branches for arms as though he were fighting for a rebound, and create space for himself.

"My style was a lot of movement off the ball," he said. "Back in those days, you could head-slap. I'd swing my arms over and under—like basketball moves. The offensive linemen weren't used to those moves. My objective was to make things happen back on their side of the line of scrimmage."

And that's what Bacon did on December 12, 1976, at Shea Stadium. He sacked Jets quarterback Joe Namath four times en route to a 42-3 Bengals victory, the same day cornerback Ken Riley snared three interceptions.

Quarterbacks such as Fran Tarkenton, Roger Staubach, Ken Stabler, and Terry Bradshaw drove Bacon crazy. But Namath's lack of mobility because of bad knees made him an easy target.

"Those other guys were tough to catch up with," Bacon said. "Tarkenton would run way down the field, come back and throw the ball on you. He'd run you all over the place. But Namath was just another quarterback who had to go down. That's all it was."

The Rams' Fearsome Foursome of the 1960s consisted of ends Deacon Jones and Lamar Lundy, and tackles Merlin Olsen and Roosevelt Grier. Bacon took over for Lundy and the combination of Roger Brown and Diron Talbert replaced Grier as the second wave of the Fearsome Foursome washed over the league.

Why did Bacon choose to make his career a cross-country tour?

"It was all about money," he said. "Teams didn't want to pay that money.

They're just throwing it out there now, but back in those days you had to fight for everything."

To get a great player, you have to give up one, and that's what transpired between the Bengals and San Diego Chargers on April 2, 1976. First-year head coach Bill "Tiger" Johnson got Paul Brown's blessing to obtain Bacon, so the Bengals pulled off a controversial trade, dealing wide receiver Charlie Joiner to the Chargers.

While Bacon's tenure in Cincinnati was brief, but memorable, Joiner—a Bengal from 1972-75—played 11 seasons for the Chargers (1976-'86) and was inducted into the Pro Football Hall of Fame in 1996 with 750 receptions for 12,146 yards and 65 TDs over an 18-year, 239-game career that began in Houston in 1969.

What does Bacon want Bengals fans to remember about him?

"My sacks," he said. "We had a bunch in '76."

Forty-six to be exact.

It was a team record that stood until the 2001 squad piled up 48.

(Bacon, 61, lives in Ironton and is a corrections officer in the Department of Youth Services at the Ohio River Valley Juvenile Corrections Facility in Franklin Furnace, Ohio. His hobby is golf.)

From Harvard, With Love

¶Pat McInally, punter, wide receiver (1976-'85)

Pat McInally has the distinction of being the only Harvard graduate to participate in both a Pro Bowl and a Super Bowl. He's also the only player who could make Bengals head coach Forrest Gregg laugh. Gregg called for his players to wear belts to team meetings. So McInally showed up in a belt—and nothing else. Greg announced he wanted his players to dress up for road trips. So McInally wore a tuxedo—top hat, tails, and cane—an entire weekend. Said Gregg: "Pat was smarter than any of us and had a great sense of humor. He knew where the parameters were, and he always pushed 'em. But he pushed 'em in a way where it was really hard for me to get mad at him."

College:
Harvard
Hometown:
Villa Park,
California
Height: 6-6,
Weight: 212
Pro Bowl: 1

McInally, a fifth-round draft pick in 1975 who spent his rookie year on injured reserve after suffering a broken leg in the College All-Stars vs. Pittsburgh Steelers game, pulled double duty as a punter and receiver during his 10-year reign as the Bengals' goofy, long-haired Ivy-Leaguer.

In 149 career games, he punted 700 times for 29,307 yards—a 41.9 average that ranks third in franchise history behind Dave Lewis (43.7 from 1970-'73) and Lee Johnson (43.2 from 1988-'98)—and caught 57 passes for 808 yards (14.2) and five touchdowns.

"I couldn't have picked a city that treated me better," said McInally, who earned a Pro Bowl bid as a punter in the 1981 Super Bowl season. "My legacy? I was a happy guy. I had a lot of fun."

But there wasn't anything funny about the events of December 21, 1980, at Riverfront Stadium when Cleveland free safety Thom Darden

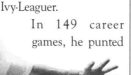

McInally, an All-American at Harvard, is the only NFL player to score a perfect 50 on the Wonderlic test, which was designed to measure general mental ability.

102

103

knocked McInally unconscious on a play known as "The Hit." McInally returned from the vicious tackle in the second quarter and late in the game caught a 59-yard TD pass from Jack Thompson. The Browns won, 27-24, on Don Cockroft's 22-yard field goal with 1:25 remaining, but McInally earned a prominent place in Cincinnati folklore for his heroic and courageous performance.

Many of the 50,058 spectators thought McInally was paralyzed by "The Hit," which is the most memorable play in the "Battle of Ohio" series because it defined the intensity of the rivalry.

"He almost got decapitated," Bengals guard Dave Lapham said. "We thought he was dead," Browns receiver Dave Logan added. The Bengals had spread the field with four wideouts and McInally was lined up in a three-man cluster to the left. When McInally released to the inside, over the middle, Darden was waiting.

"I ran into both of his forearms," McInally said. Darden, president of an investment company in Cedar Rapids, Iowa, said he remembers the play "like it was yesterday.

"We had a coverage designed for that specific play where I would fake going deep-middle, then come up in the linebacker area," Darden said. "As fate would have it, they ran the exact play we were looking for, like you drew it up on the board.

McInally, in training camp in 1981, showed that he was bilingual—he could catch the ball as well as kick it.

To have the type of personality to make
**Forrest
Gregg** laugh
at what
you're doing
was quite a
feat in
itself.

—Jim
LeClair

"McInally comes underneath. Jack Thompson doesn't even see me. I have a decision to make. Do I go for the ball or do I go for him because we were all three meeting at the same time. I decided I was going for him because I couldn't get to the ball."

McInally lay motionless, having swallowed his tongue. "That's what scared me the most," Darden said. "I stood over him until one of their guards knocked me down. They had to come out and pull his tongue out. Once I saw that he could breathe, I felt much better."

Darden thought he had hit McInally in the chest. "But after reviewing the film, I hit him in the chest and my forearm went up and I hit him underneath his neck."

The late *Dayton Daily News* sports editor Si Burick wrote: "McInally was deathly still for some 10 minutes. Stretched across the cart like a dead horse, he was wheeled off. Neck damage. We all feared the worst. Talk about a miracle. With some four minutes remaining in the second quarter, there were the Bengals in a punting situation. And who came out from the sideline with the kicking unit to handle his other assignment as the team's punter? The dead man, McInally, that's who."

McInally had regained all his feeling in the locker room and decided to play. When he walked out of the

McInally and a fan participate in an 1982 training camp demonstration of how the Ivy League is still capable of small talk.

tunnel and onto the field, the crowd exploded in applause.

"Obviously, it was a big thrill to come back and catch a touchdown," McInally said. "Having Forrest Gregg

knocked out. He might or might not be able to play.' Pat just wouldn't have it any other way. I'll tell you one thing right now. A lot of times, it's tough to get people on the field, and when you've got people who want to get on, you have a tendency to listen to 'em."

Darden said he's never spoken to McInally since "The Hit." "The first thing I'd say to him is that I'm glad he was OK, then I'd be mad at him because he came back and caught a touchdown pass," Darden said.

"Obviously, I'd want him to know that's the way we were taught and we were drilled as defensive backs. If a player comes into your area, the ball is as much yours as it is theirs. If you can't get the ball, you hit the receiver. It was nothing personal."

Looking back, Darden said he was "really beaten up pretty bad in the papers about that play. But I think it all worked out. We won the game, the league got its money on my fine, and Pat McInally got his health."

(McInally, 51, created the "Starting Lineup" toy line of action figures for Kenner, which earned him millions in royalties. He is also the founder of Good Sports for Life, a program dedicated to helping parents improve youth sports. The California-based McInally also writes a column for NFL.com.)

ask at halftime if I'd play again after being knocked out was an interesting experience. It was pretty amazing that they allowed me to play. If a boxer was knocked out for 25 or 30 minutes, he wouldn't have come back and fought with the opposition."

Said Gregg: "I asked the doctors, 'Is he OK?' They said, 'Well, he's

> I was a ball hawk. The action was where the ball was, and that's where I wanted to be.
>
> —Reggie Williams

108

Samurai Linebacker

¶Reggie Williams, linebacker (1976-'89)

With a body like a bronze god, Reggie Williams' affinity for Far East culture was triggered by his trip to the Japan Bowl college all-star game in 1976 and led to the Yin Yang tattoo emblazoned on the inside of his right forearm. The black and white figure symbolizes the balance of life—darkness and light, positive and negative. "It is my power button," Williams said. "Whenever I was fatigued or hurt or needed to focus, I always looked at that one spot," he said. "It was a way of erasing the negativity of a George Hill." And a Bo Schembechler.

College: Dartmouth
Hometown: Flint, Michigan
Height: 6-0, Weight: 230

Those two Big Ten coaches—Schembechler, the head coach at Michigan, and Hill, the defensive coordinator at Ohio State under Woody Hayes—could have destroyed him. Instead, their words and deeds only served as motivation for Williams, who became Dartmouth's first NFL player, a two-time Super Bowl participant, and 14-year starter at right outside linebacker for the Bengals.

He ranks second in franchise history with 62.5 sacks, including a team-high 11 in 1981. "I ended up at Dartmouth because Bo Schembechler told me to my face I wasn't good enough to be a Wolverine," Williams said. But that was nothing compared to the shabby treatment he received from Hill at the Hula Bowl all-star game in Hawaii after Williams' brilliant college career at the Ivy League school in Hanover, N.H.

Nearly 30 years after Hula Bowl Hell Week,

Williams—a former Cincinnati city councilman—is one of only three NFL players holding public office before retirement. The others: Lions back Yale Lary and 49ers tackle Bob St. Clair.

109

Williams hasn't forgotten. "George Hill treated me as an inconvenience and let me know, in his opinion, there was no place at the next level for an Ivy League linebacker," Williams said. "He actually had almost convinced me that I wasn't good enough to play in the NFL. In practice, he asked me to go get water for the other players. During the pregame speech, he had said a joke in which I was the punchline. And when he put me in the game, he said, 'The only reason I'm putting you in the game is because I have to.' And he only put me in one play."

Hill had screamed, "This is Big Ten football! Not Pac-8!" Then he looked at Williams and everyone laughed. The message: If the Pac-8 was bad, the Ivy League was nothing.

The next time Williams saw Hill was in 1979, at Riverfront Stadium. The Bengals would finish 4-12 and the Eagles 11-5, but that day belonged to Cincinnati—a 37-13 victory. Williams caused two fumbles, one on the opening kickoff and another on a screen pass. He stunned Ohio State teammates Archie Griffin and Pete Johnson by yelling at Hill before the game.

"I remember running up the sideline after I created the first fumble, and I ran over to (Hill)

and said, 'I'm not done yet!' "

Williams lives by a simple philosophy: All or none. And the roots of his unbridled passion and intensity for football can be traced to his youth, when a hearing defect led to his placement in a school for the deaf and dumb. With the help of lip reading and concentration, he persevered, overcame, and succeeded.

He memorized British author William Earnest Henley's 1875 poem, "Invictus," which concludes with the lines: "I am the master of my fate; I am the captain of my soul." He studied the teachings of samurai warrior Miyamoto Musashi, who lived by this code: "When you sacrifice your life, you must make the fullest use of your weaponry. It is false not to do so, and to die with a weapon yet undrawn."

And he forced himself to suffer during training camps at Wilmington College, living like a Buddhist monk. No air conditioning, TV or radio. Just a shoulder

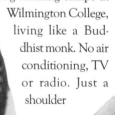

bag containing clothes, a box of books, and a clock so as to avoid the $100-a-minute fines for tardiness. And he slept on the floor.

Williams figured the masochism was worth it. Enduring 90-plus-degree heat in an upstairs sauna of a dorm room gave him a jump-start on the punishment he would absorb during the season. Opponents such as Cleveland Browns halfback Earnest Byner and Houston Oilers wide receiver Ken Burrough hated him because of his flying elbows, ferocious forearms, and tornado-like tackles, which causes Williams to smile with fiendish delight.

"It was not in my job description," he said, "to have my opponents like me." Although the sportswriter consensus was that he played one of the finest games of his career in Super Bowl XXIII when he registered one of four Bengals' sacks against Joe Montana, Williams basks in the memory of two games from his 1976 rookie season—his first action on defense, a 45-24 victory at Cleveland, and a 27-7 triumph in his first career start, in the Astrodome at Houston.

"The most emotionally impactful game was the first game I came off the bench," he said. "I grew up a Browns fan. Jim Brown was my idol and to fulfill the dream of playing on the same field as Jim Brown, it reverberates to this day."

The Oilers had an explosive offense featuring quarterback Dan Pastorini and wide receivers Billy "White Shoes" Johnson and Burrough. Williams' assignment was to make Burrough's life miserable, and he did, teaming with cornerback Ken "The Rattler" Riley to shut down the man who wore uniform number "00."

"Reggie was very energetic and sort of wild on the field," Riley said. "We wanted to be physical with Kenny. So I told Reggie, 'Every time he comes off the line, really jam him, bump him, and push him around.' Kenny and I worked out together in the

> He did throw a couple of elbows, but that's all right. Reggie had intensity that hasn't been rivaled by many players. You could count on him all the time. He was going to come prepared.
>
> —Jim LeClair

offseason, and he came up to me and said : 'Rattler, that number 57, is he crazy?' I said, 'Yeah, you've got to be careful with him because that guy *is* crazy.'

"I went back and told Reggie, 'Keep hitting him, Reggie, keep hitting him.' Kenny could really run, but he didn't want to come across the middle." Recalled Reggie: "It was the Old West in football. Hitting, gouging, head-slaps—anything went. I was obviously energized, starting my first game. He was a big target and I had fast forearms, and there was no limitation on how many times you hit a guy and for how long. That was one of the few games he didn't catch a ball. I heard the Houston players talking to Rattler: 'What's wrong with that guy?' All I listened to was Ken Riley saying, 'Keep doing it. Keep doing it.'"

Williams' contributions off the field were plentiful, too. He served as a Cincinnati city councilman from May 1988 until December 1990 when he resigned and became general manager of the New York/New Jersey Knights of the World League of American Football, the forerunner to NFL Europe, from 1991-'92. He then went to work for the NFL, organizing a youth education and recreation center in south-central Los Angeles. In April 1993, he was appointed director of sports development at Walt Disney World theme park. Each tackle, sack, feeling, emotion, and job served as a layer of experience, molding Williams into a man whose spirit is unshakable, unsinkable and, most of all—to borrow a word from "Invictus"—unconquerable.

"I optimistically like to look at ourselves as always in the state of becoming the person we are," Williams said. "Life is a wonderful journey of enlightenment."

(Williams, 49, is vice president of Disney Sports Attractions in Orlando, Florida, with responsibility for all the sports facilities, water parks, and golf courses at Walt Disney World. His hobbies are reading, photography, and collecting art.)

> **I can remember running a route near Williams and him elbowing me for no reason. I hated him as a football player from that day forward.**
>
> —Browns tailback Earnest Byner

113

Heart and Soul

¶Eddie Edwards, defensive end (1977-'88)

The wild, Don King-style electric hair is long gone. Eddie Edwards has a shaved head. "I've got the clean-cut look," he said. "My head looks like a basketball." He may look different, but he's still the same fun-loving guy, locker-room comedian, and terrific teammate he's always been. It's just that he wears a hard hat now instead of a helmet. It's appropriate that he's employed in the construction industry because he was a blue-collar player who gave eight hours' work for eight hours' pay.

College: Miami of Florida
Hometown: Fort Pierce, Florida
Height: 6-5, Weight:258

Edwards clocked in with the Bengals in 1977 as the draft's No. 3 overall pick in the first round from the University of Miami, and clocked out as the club's career leader with 83.5 quarterback sacks. Light for a defensive end—265 pounds was the most he ever weighed—"Double E" had the kind of mobility, agility, and hostility that gave offensive tackles nightmares.

"I was a speed rusher," he said. "I made guys respect my speed. I liked to get a guy moving and beat him off the corner. Then once I showed 'em some speed, I tried to go 'up and in' on 'em. When I first came into the league, the swim move was big. I'd just head-butt a guy, jerk 'em one way and swim over. That was my favorite move. But then the league changed, and so did my technique of the game. Offensive linemen got a chance to get their hands on you, so I had to change my style of rushing. But I always relied on my speed."

The Bengals ran a 3-4 scheme and Edwards, a left end, was the cornerstone of the famed "WEB" defensive front that included nose tackle Wilson Whitley and right end Ross Browner. Edwards led the team in sacks in 1980 (12),

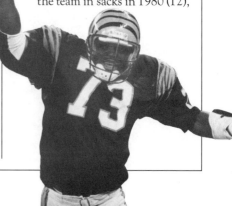

Edwards was light for a defensive end but his heart kept him in play, making him one of the great—and underrated—Bengal defensive linemen.

Skip Peterson

115

1981 (10) and 1983 (13), and he owns the franchise single-game record with five sacks, against Cleveland's Brian Sipe on December 21, 1980, at Riverfront Stadium. "That game, it was like everything my coach was telling me to do, I did, and it worked," Edwards said. "A lot of those sacks, I just ran the guy down. He was scrambling and I was quick."

The other game that sticks in his mind was the Bengals' 24-10 victory over the visiting Los Angeles Rams on November 15, 1981, when he knocked out quarterback Dan Pastorini. Edwards was under severe pressure to perform well that game because he overslept the day before and got fined for missing the team's 7 p.m. Saturday meeting at a Cincinnati hotel. He didn't arrive until 10 p.m.

"I set my clock to a.m. instead of p.m.," he said. "The coaches even came by my house. They were all worried about me. I was just knocked out sleeping. Man, I was in hot water. Forrest Gregg was the kind of coach that put the fear in you if you didn't play good on Sunday. I had to get my shit together in a hurry."

Edwards did. He sacked Pastorini twice, and recalled how the second hit was enough to send the quarterback to the hospital with a concussion: "I got by my man and Pastorini kind of tucked his head down. I ran into him, hit him with my chest and he just bounced backward, and his head hit against the turf. He got up and was all wobbly. Two guys carried him off. He was through for the game."

Who knows how many sacks Edwards would've generated had he played 12 years in a defensive alignment with a four-man front? In the linebacker-oriented 3-4 defense, he constantly fought double teams. He'd beat the right tackle only to have the right guard waiting on him.

"If you had a four-man line, oh, man, once you beat your guy, you don't have anybody else to worry about unless they had a running back waiting there to chip you," he said. "To get a sack in the 3-4, you often had to go around the outside.

"But I'm still proud of my career. I've always been a hard worker. I dedicated myself in trying not to look bad. Even though we may have been three touchdowns behind, I never quit. I was still doing my job to the end."

(Edwards, 50, works as a supervisor for ABC Cutting Contractors, Inc., a concrete-cutting business in Pompano Beach, Florida. His hobbies are fishing and lifting weights. "A lot of guys figured, once I got out of football, I'd balloon up to 300 pounds. Right now I'm at 248. I'm still in pretty good shape. I've never had that problem of gaining weight.")

Eddie Edwards was a great pass rusher. He just kept doing it game in and game out, and never got the credit he deserved. That was the case sometimes.

—Jim LeClair

117

The Bulldozer

¶Pete Johnson, fullback (1977-'83)

There was absolutely no way Pete Johnson was going to play another season for the Bengals for a measly $100,000. Not after leading the team in rushing for seven straight seasons and scoring 70 touchdowns, a franchise record that still stands. A hundred grand? Heck, that was chump change for ol' Pete, who topped that figure as a car salesman in the offseason. So he up and quit—sort of—in 1984.

College: Ohio State. Hometown: Fort Valley, Georgia Height: 6-0, Weight: 249 Pro Bowl: 1

Johnson told the Bengals he wasn't going to report to training camp under new head coach Sam Wyche, so they shipped him to San Diego for tailback James Brooks on May 29, 1984. Turns out it was the best trade in Bengals history because Brooks became the franchise rushing leader (6,447) until Corey Dillon shattered the mark in 2002. But Johnson also got what he wanted—out from underneath Paul Brown's thumb.

He didn't last long in San Diego. The Chargers traded him to Miami in September, and he spent '84 with the Dolphins, where he earned $280,000, then retired. To this day, Johnson swears the Bengals didn't want him to score in Super Bowl XVI because of the Almighty Dollar. Johnson was held to 36 yards on 14 carries with a long gain of 5 yards that grim day in Pontiac, Michigan, when the mistake-prone Bengals succumbed to the San Francisco 49ers, 26-21, at the Silverdome.

Johnson was a 6-foot bulldozer whose weight fluctuated between 249 and 260. But he was stopped short of the end zone twice from 1 yard out during the 49ers' famous goal-line stand late in the third quarter that allowed them to cling to a 20-7 lead. "We ran left all season behind (tackle) Anthony Munoz," Johnson said. "But they (the coaches) wanted to do the right side for some strange reason. Who knows? I have my ideas."

It was money, honey.

"Yup," he said. "When you score in the Super Bowl, that's a big deal. (The Bengals) don't want you to get superstar status because they don't want to pay you."

Johnson went to Ohio State to play linebacker, then found himself at fullback. When he carried the ball, he said, he "went into a trance."

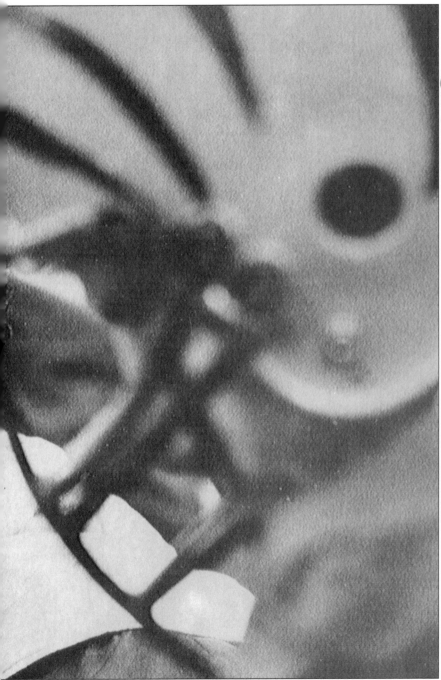

Charles Steinbrunner

121

Johnson remembers Wyche calling him in Columbus and asking him to sign in '84. "I said, 'Sam, I played seven years and they ain't paid me yet, and they've been promising me they're going to pay me. I was told to just be quiet and they'll pay me. And I did.' I told him, 'They ain't going to give it to me now.'

"It ain't like I was a slouch. I got better every year. I led the team in rushing and scoring (TDs) every year. I said, 'They ain't going to pay me. They don't pay. They've got a history of that.'

"He asked me on the phone, 'Well, how much money do you want? You've got to be making $500,000.' I told him, 'I'll come in for $350,000.' He said, 'I know I can get that. C'mon in.' I said, 'No. I'm not coming in.' That's when he asked me to meet with him. I wouldn't come to Cincinnati. I told him where I'd meet him—halfway."

So Johnson and Wyche met at a truck stop in Washington Court House to hash out their differences.

The Dozer on adversity: "I'm just like a rechargeable battery; the worse things get, the better I am."

An agreement was nearly reached. "Sam said, 'C'mon, let's go back now.' I told him, 'If you get it ($350,000), you call me and I'll be there. But I'm not going to pack my bag yet.' This was on a Friday. Then I read in the paper the next Monday, 'If Pete don't want to play for the Bengals, we don't want him.'"

Johnson idolized his coach at Ohio State, Woody Hayes, so it was only natural that he adored Bengals head coach Forrest Gregg. "Woody said when he gave you the ball, he's trusting you with the family jewels and you've got to protect 'em," Johnson said.

"So when I got the ball, the only thing on my mind was scoring. I was faster than most of the defensive backs I played against. I've never been caught from behind without scoring."

Hayes told Johnson when the Bengals grabbed him in the second round of

122

the 1977 NFL Draft: "You've got to take that same intensity you had in college and take it to the pros. If you do, you'll have no trouble making the team."

Fellow Bengals running back Lenvil Elliott taught Johnson how to pace himself. "When I first came into the league, I had made the team and I did just like Woody said," Johnson said. "I'm diving and jumping over piles and all this stuff.

"And Lenvil pulled me to the side and said, 'Son, if you never listen to another word I say, remember this: 'Once your body leaves the ground, it don't belong to you anymore.' I said, 'OK, I got it.'

"Woody always used to say, 'Each man is better than he himself thinks he is.' And that was one of Forrest's philosophies. He'll get it out of you, buddy. He'd say: 'When you're out on that field, you should be giving 100-plus. And when you're off the field, you rest.' I look at these guys today and they run 20 yards, and then they're over on the sidelines with oxygen on 'em. It's all specialty positions now.

"Forrest just was the greatest," Johnson added. "I put him in the Woody Hayes category. One day, Forrest came to me and said, 'I think I got you some help.'

"I said, 'Yeah, coach? What are you talking about? What do you got, another running back?' He said, 'No, no, no, no, no. I got this kid from USC coming. Let me tell you something. I was trying to test his blocking style to see if he could pass block. I went to do a little rush on him and he knocked me right on my ass. He's a good one.' I said, 'All right!'"

It was, of course, Munoz, who would eventually be enshrined in the Pro Football Hall of Fame in Canton.

Johnson said he still gets a thousand fan letters a month, just like when he played. He can still hear fans chanting his name.

"I usually was the first one to get to the stadium and the last one to leave. There was a crowd at the locker room before the game and there was a crowd there when I left. The fans and I had a great relationship. I was one of those guys who could've played another four or five years. But I went out on top."

(Johnson, 50, is a self-proclaimed workaholic who mans three jobs in the Columbus, Ohio, area. He owns Fourth and One Enterprises, a sports promotions company specializing in banquets and golf outings; operates Professional Sports Management as a licensed sports agent; and leases cars to pro athletes nationwide for Thompson and Ward, an automobile leasing company. His hobbies: "Golf, golf, and golf," he said.)

123

Master of Disguise

¶Louis Breeden, cornerback (1978-'87)

Teammates loved to tease cornerback Louis Breeden about his hands. At times, they were pillow-soft mitts. Other times, they were hands of stone. Either question marks or exclamation points. If Louis caught half the interceptions he dropped, his Bengal buddies say, he would've shattered Ken Riley's team-record 65. OK, so some balls slithered through his fingertips and kissed the carpet. Sweet Lou is a legend because of the ones he gathered in.

College: North Carolina Central
Hometown: Hamlet, N.C.
Height: 5-11
Weight: 185

He made plenty of pretty plays during a 10-year career in which he picked off 33 enemy passes—second only to Riley in club history—but one stands alone in Bengals lore.

It came on November 8, 1981, at San Diego Jack Murphy Stadium in a 40-17 victory over the Chargers. With San Diego in the shadow of the Bengals' goal line and the outcome still in doubt, Breeden pulled a Houdini, picking off a Dan Fouts pass intended for Charlie Joiner and sailing 102 yards down the left sideline for a touchdown—the longest play in franchise history.

The record has been tied twice, courtesy of Eric Bieniemy's kickoff return against the New York Giants at the Meadowlands (October 26, 1997) and Artrell Hawkins' interception at Houston (November 3, 2002). But Breeden's magic came during the stretch run to the Super Bowl. "San Diego had that great offense," Breeden said. "They were like a tornado, man. If they had scored, it would've given them some momentum. You know how momentum works. It gives you confidence.

"Well, we had played a lot of man-to-man that game. But we disguised our coverage real well. We were playing zone and that zone looked like it was man."

As the left cornerback, Breeden was lined up across from Chargers wide receiver Wes Chandler. Fouts wanted Chandler to run a curl into the end zone and take Breeden out of the play. That would allow Joiner, the slot receiver, to score on a quick-out route in the unoccupied area on the right

Breeden was one of the league's top cornerbacks. And his 102-yard interception runback is still the longest play in franchise history.

124

A bundle of nervous energy, Breeden hated sitting on the bench during games. "The coach would call us over and I'm like, 'Damn, coach, I'm missing the ball game.'

Charles Steinbrunner

125

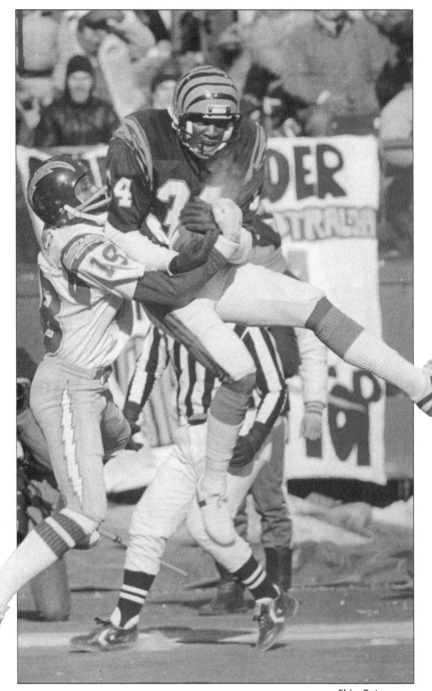

Skip Peterson

126

side. "I played it like it was man, and all I did was hang on the inside watching the quarterback," Breeden said.

"He thought I was going to run off, but I didn't. I stepped in front of it and made the pick. If I had dropped that one, everybody on the team deserved to come and slay me in the stadium. But Fouts threw it too well for me to drop it. Once I caught it, it was clear sailing.

"It was just a quick read and a three-step drop. Fouts threw it expecting one thing and he didn't get what he thought he was getting."

The Bengals got a superb player when they picked Breeden in the seventh round of the 1977 draft. After sitting out his rookie year on injured reserve, he broke into the starting lineup in '78 after Lemar Parrish's exit to Washington.

With a little help from Isaac Curtis, Breeden wrestled the starting job away from Melvin Morgan in training camp. "Everyone was sort of in awe of Isaac," Breeden said. "He was the kind of receiver who made everybody nervous because he was a Pro Bowler, world class sprinter, and very difficult to cover. They had me behind Ken Riley on the right side and the headlines were: 'Breeden challenging Riley for starting spot.'

"After covering Isaac on a particular play, we were both going by Charley Winner, our defensive backs coach. Isaac said, in not such a subtle way, but in an emphatic way, 'You've got your best two corners on the same side.' It was only a little while later that they moved me to the left side."

Breeden remembers getting beat by Pittsburgh's Lynn Swann for five catches for 78 yards and a 12-yard TD in a 28-3 Steelers' win in Cincinnati in '78. In the return match at Three Rivers Stadium, Breeden shut out Swann (zero catches); picked off two Terry Bradshaw passes; and nearly KO'd halfback Rocky Bleier.

"He ran a little flair route," Breeden said. "Bradshaw dumped it off to him and it was maybe the best hit I had as a professional. I ran up and smacked him, and he let the ball go. I got up and he laid on the ground for a moment, but he eventually got up."

Like a phoenix rising from the North Carolina sandhills, Breeden emerged as one of the league's top corners. He doesn't run anymore because of nagging back pain, but his ball-hawking hands are still remembered—and respected.

(Breeden, 51, owns Louis Breeden Promotions, an advertising specialty company, in the Cincinnati area. His No. 1 hobby is playing golf with ex-Bengals Isaac Curtis, Barney Bussey, David Fulcher, and John Simmons. "I'm the sheriff and those guys are my deputies," he said.)

Unsung Hero

¶*Steve Kreider, wide receiver (1979-'86)*

You don't graduate with an electrical engineering degree from Lehigh University without brains. And you don't survive eight years in the NFL without brawn. Steve Kreider had both. Other guys were stronger. Still others were swifter. But when it came to reading defensive schemes, Kreider processed information quickly and had a knack for finding holes in the secondary. Then he'd cradle the ball as though it were a newborn and run like mad.

College: Lehigh Hometown: Reading, Pennsylvania Height: 6-3, Weight: 192

Kreider was versatility, wrapped in reliability, tucked inside dependability. A terrific No. 3 wide receiver after being selected in the sixth round (139th overall) of the 1979 draft, he emerged as the perfect complement to starters Isaac Curtis and Cris Collinsworth because you could flank him, split him, or slot him. He was a change of pace. A key outlet on third down. A role player. An unsung hero beloved by his teammates.

"I don't think of myself in the legend category, to tell you the truth," Kreider said. "But I'd like to be remembered as a guy who delivered when the chips were down. I just tried to catch it when they threw it to me.

"I was lucky because I played on a good team. Kenny Anderson and Boomer Esiason were both really good passers. That was a good pass offense to be a part of. They were both awfully good."

And so was Kreider. He caught 150 passes for 2,119 yards (a 14.1-yard average) and nine touchdowns in 114 career games. His best season was 1981 when his 37 grabs for 520

Kreider (at far right), catches game-winning TD at Pittsburgh (17-10), as Bengals head for Super Bowl.

128

yards and five TDs served as catalysts on the drive to the Super Bowl.

Surely the victory over San Diego for the AFC championship and the Super Bowl loss to the 49ers are his favorite memories, right?

Wrong.

It's the Bengals' sweep of Pittsburgh in '81–a 34-7 victory at Riverfront on October 18, then a 17-10 triumph at Three Rivers on December 13 that clinched the AFC Central Division title. In the first meeting that year, Kreider

caught a pass on a go-route during a first-quarter TD drive "that maybe helped light the fire," he said.

"That was a situation where you had a team that had not won before and was wondering whether it could. You had some players on that team who wanted to light the fire and make everybody believe. If one or two guys can make a play, pretty soon you've got momentum."

Kreider caught a TD pass in the second half of the return matchup in Pittsburgh "that I think was an exclamation point for us. Those were situations where I was at the right spot at the right time and it was really fun to be a part of that."

More stagehand than headliner, Kreider didn't often step out of the shadows of his more-publicized

Whatever you wanted Steve to do, he was there. QB for the scout squad, holder for extra points and field goals, whatever. We did a thing at the Montgomery Inn for our 'Most Valuable Beaver'— the guy who did the most. He won it every year."

—Pete Johnson

teammates. But when he got the opportunity to climb on stage, he seized the spotlight and his star burned with a brilliant fire. Told he was a Bengals "great" for his outstanding contribution and consummate professionalism, he shifted into the self-deprecating mode.

"It's amazing," he said. "Is that 50 legends or a million and 50?"

Typical Steve Kreider. Corralling him on the telephone and getting him to open up and talk about himself was similar to what cornerbacks faced trying to cover him—a challenge.

(Kreider, 46, is managing director with Morgan Stanley & Co. in Philadelphia. He manages money for institutional clients. "My number one hobby is beating Cris (Collinsworth) in golf. But it's hard. He's a little better than I am. Tell him he needs to give me strokes.")

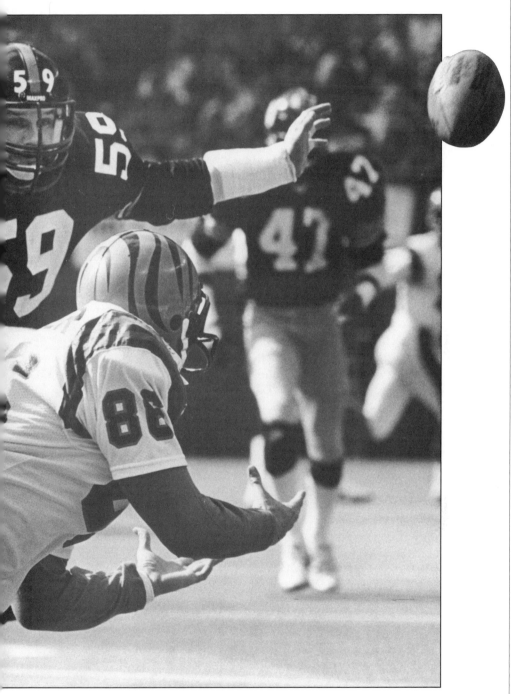

Skip Peterson (left) and Doug Lewis

Mighty Max

¶Max Montoya, guard (1979-'89)

Max Montoya will be the first to admit he never looked particularly impressive or imposing in a sweat-soaked T-shirt and shorts. But decorate him with a football uniform and he's Clark Kent emerging from a telephone booth with an "S" on his chest. When it came to playing guard for the Bengals, nobody did it better than Montoya.

College:
UCLA
Hometown:
La Puente,
California
Height: 6-5,
Weight: 275
Pro Bowls: 3

He pulled with quickness and precision, clearing paths for running backs off tackle and around end, and was a shutdown pass protector for 11 seasons until his controversial exit to the Los Angeles Raiders.

"Pulling was probably one of my favorite things as an offensive guard, leading the running back around the corner," Montoya said. "The thing I liked about it was you had to do sight adjustments on the run based on the defense and the coverage. You generally had a pre-assigned cornerback or outside 'backer or safety you had to take out depending on the defense, so I enjoyed kind of reading things on the run."

A seventh-round steal in 1979 out of UCLA, where he played offensive tackle—flip-flopping to the open side opposite the tight end—Montoya could be a good trivia question. Who were Barney Cotton, James White, Vaughn Lusby, and Casey Merrill? All were drafted by the Bengals that year before they plucked Mighty Max with the 168th pick. All Montoya accomplished was three trips to the Pro Bowl and a starting berth in a pair of Super Bowls.

How could so many teams miss the boat on such a quality player? Because they failed to realize that, behind the jersey, beat the heart of a champion.

"Everybody in the league is tough and pretty damn quick," Montoya said. "But maybe I had good feet, somewhat of a good balance that kept me going, and the will to get things done. I don't know what it is that makes a particular player stand out. But whatever it is, I suppose, maybe I had some of it."

One of Montoya's most memorable games was a 50-35 loss at San Diego in 1982—a Monday night. Ken Anderson threw for 416 yards and

When Montoya left for Los Angeles—the most high-profile, free-agent loss in Bengals history—it was also a harbinger for the dark Cincinnati decade that lay ahead.

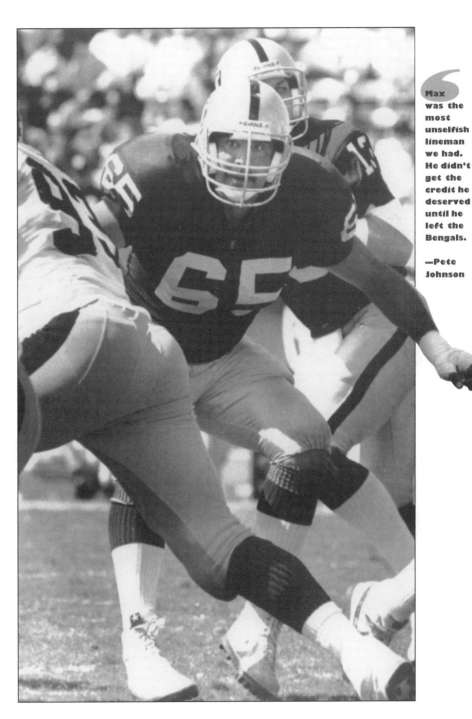

Max was the most unselfish lineman we had. He didn't get the credit he deserved until he left the Bengals.

—Pete Johnson

two TDs, and Montoya battled Chargers defensive tackle Louie Kelcher. "My body was completely drained. Playing against Big Lou, a massive 325-pound guy back in the early '80s—a guy like that was uncommon."

As outstanding as he was as a player, Montoya was an even better businessman. And that's why he high-tailed it to Los Angeles as the most high-profile, free-agent loss in Bengals history, courtesy of the "Plan B" free agent system. The Bengals underestimated his value around the league, and it cost them his services.

Under the Plan B structure, teams protected their finest 37 players, exposing the others to free agency. Montoya verbally agreed to take a $25,000 bonus if he spurned any offers and remained a Bengal, so the club gambled and left him unprotected—a big mistake.

"At the time, the Bengals placed several players on Plan B, where you had the opportunity to look at other teams," Montoya said. "So the Bengals were making deals: 'We'll give you so much money if you don't go anywhere.' They approached me with it. I said, 'No problem.' I talked with Mike Brown about it.

"He said, 'I don't think you're going to go anywhere.' I said, 'Well, I will at least talk to people.' That's how we left it. Lo and behold, a lot of people came looking at me. I wasn't looking to leave anywhere."

Montoya was at the Pro Bowl in Hawaii when the telephone rang. It was Raiders owner Al Davis on the line. "He personally called me and set up some arrangements," Montoya said.

"I talked to them. I was hoping the Bengals would call me back, but I guess they never called, and I was gone. I have no regrets at all. It was just one of those things where I had a chance to go back home and play before my family and friends where I grew up.

"It was a hard thing leaving the Bengals and all my buddies back here, but it worked out fine for me because I played another five years (1990-'94) and made another Pro Bowl ('93)."

Montoya was viewed by some Bengals fans as a traitor for leaving, but that's what free agency is all about. Nothing personal. Just business. He considered relocating on the West Coast, but loved Cincinnati enough to stay and call it home.

(Montoya, 48, owns and operates three Penn Station East Coast Subs stores in Northern Kentucky. He lives on a 50-acre farm in Hebron, Kentucky, where he indulges in his No. 1 hobby—horses. "I'm a city kid with horses," Montoya said.)

> **I hear** that a lot. That when I left, they never could get outside again. They've not had a guard that can pull like that.
>
> —Max Montoya

Chance Brockway

135

Dan the Man

¶Dan Ross, tight end (1979-'83,'85)

The Bengals, Buffalo Bills, and Chicago Bears did what many considered unthinkable and unpardonable in the 1979 NFL Draft. All three teams passed on tight end Kellen Winslow—twice—before he went to the San Diego Chargers with the 13th overall pick. The Bengals had their reasons. They thought it was time to replenish the quarterback and running back positions, so they took Jack Thompson—"The Throwin' Samoan"—and Charles Alexander Nos. 3 and 12. They also knew they could get the tight end they wanted in the second round. They figured right.

College: Northeastern
Hometown: Saugus, Massachusetts
Height: 6-4,
Weight: 235
Pro Bowls: 1

Bengals assistant general manager Mike Brown went to scout Joe Senser of West Chester (Pa.) University in the fall of '78, but returned to Cincinnati raving about Northeastern's Dan Ross, who outshined Senser in a head-to-head matchup.

Ross ran disciplined routes. He showed incredible concentration. He had unbelievable hands. With the 30th pick, the Bengals made Dan their man, and for six seasons, he made them proud of their bold decision to pass on a future Hall of Famer in Winslow and take

a chance on a tough-as-nails kid with a thick New England accent and blue-collar work ethic.

Ross' 11 receptions—good for 104 yards and two touchdowns—against San Francisco in Super Bowl XVI at the Pontiac Silverdome on January 24, 1982, remains a Super Bowl record, tied with the 49ers' Jerry Rice, who accomplished the feat against Cincinnati in Super Bowl XXIII.

"I wasn't the fastest tight end and I wasn't the biggest tight end, but I prided myself on reading coverages well and my strength was that I very rarely made mental mistakes," Ross said.

"It seemed every year there

One of Ross' strong points was his concentration on the football. In 1981, he finished the season without dropping one ball.

I'm gonna
get hit
anyway.
I might
as well
catch it.

—Dan Ross

137

Dan Ross probably had as good a pair of hands as anybody I've ever seen. We'd run those tight end option routes where he and Kenny would have to be on the same page. It was almost like a pick and roll in basketball.

—Dave Lapham

139

was someone with more physical ability than I had coming into camp. My advantage was the mental part of the game.

"Another strong point was my concentration on the football. You hate to brag about yourself, but I did go through one year (1981) where I did not drop one ball. I thought that was pretty neat. You don't get too many opportunities to catch the ball. My theory is: 'I'm gonna get hit anyway. I might as well catch it.'"

Ross had 71 catches without a drop, good for 910 yards (a 12.8 average) and five TDs, that Super Bowl season. But he earned a prominent place in his teammates' hearts the year before when

he sprained a knee and had a tooth knocked out against Buffalo, spent the week on crutches, and played the next game at Cleveland.

"He was in the trainer's room, getting treatment that Tuesday, and it looked like he wasn't going to play the rest of the season," guard Dave Lapham said.

"We were playing the Browns that weekend. I said, 'Man, are you gonna be able to make it?' He said, 'Oh, yeah, I'll play.' The sucker went out and played. I couldn't believe it.

"We used to call him Gumby

Make a wish: Ross tries to get away from a Green Bay defender in 1983 after catching a pass from quarterback Turk Schonert.

because of how flexible he was. He'd contort his body to make catches that other people just couldn't make. Anything that was within his outstretched arms, he would catch. He had unbelievable body control on how he could twist and turn and make catches."

The chemistry between Ross and quarterback Ken Anderson was a thing of beauty to watch for Bengals fans, but a source of frustration for opponents. Ross ran option routes in which he'd read the linebacker or safety, then break to the open side, always trusting Anderson to deliver the ball in an area that was a safe cocoon.

"It was impossible to cover me one on one, not because of my athleticism by any means, but we had option routes where Kenny would go back in his drop and he'd be reading the same person I was," Ross said.

"If the man was covering me inside, I'd break outside. If the coverage was outside, he'd throw it the other way. There was a lot of trial and error, but it got to the point where we knew exactly what the other was thinking.

"There were a lot of times when I'd break a route, and he'd throw it to my left side or right side to stop me, because if he would have led me, I would have gotten killed. He had that great knack, that instinct, to throw it to the right spot. That's the reason why guys caught the ball for him.

They knew they weren't going to get strung out."

Ross' NFL career was interrupted in 1984 when he spent a season in the World Football League. He had signed a "futures contract" with the Boston Breakers only to have the franchise move to New Orleans. He returned to the Bengals in 1985, but finished the season with Seattle and moved on to Green Bay in '86. After his "ham sandwich and a cup of coffee" with the Seahawks and Packers, Ross retired with 290 catches for 3,419 yards (11.8) and 19 TDs in 104 career games, a small-school star thankful for the chance to play in the bigs.

"Just getting drafted was a thrill," he said. "You don't expect it from the school I went to. At the time, you don't expect to be playing in the National Football League, and especially somebody taking you with the 30th pick overall. It's like, 'Oh, geez, they must see something that I don't.' "

(Ross, 46, is president and co-owner of WBWP, an independent TV station in Riviera Beach, Florida, which, among other things, produces live shows and televises Florida Atlantic University football and basketball games. In early 2004, he was elected to the College Football Hall of Fame (Class of 2004). His hobbies are golf and fishing.)

❝ Ross wanted his Super Bowl record-tying 11 catches preserved, so he isn't ashamed to admit he rooted against the Patriots' Deion Branch in the 2004 Super Bowl. "Branch had 10 catches with three minutes to go. I was hoping for a fumble so Carolina would get the ball."

—Dan Ross

Foot Soldier

¶Jim Breech, placekicker (1980-'92)

College:
California
Hometown:
Sacramento,
California
Height: 5-6,
Weight:161

When the telephone rang at his El Sobrante, California, townhouse on November 25, 1980, unemployed kicker Jim Breech figured it was the Cleveland Browns on the line. After all, Browns Hall of Fame legend Paul Warfield—the club's assistant director of pro personnel—had called the previous week. "That was the year of the Kardiac Kids and Paul Warfield called me and said (Don) Cockroft's knee and back were really bad, and they weren't sure if he was going to make it through the season," Breech said. "He wanted to know if I would be willing to come out and kick or at least try out. He just told me I was the guy.

"It was the middle of the week and they said they'd fly me out over the weekend, so I was expecting a call back. But they never called. The following Tuesday when the phone rang, I thought it was them."

Nope.

It was Frank Smouse, the Bengals' assistant director of player personnel, with the call that changed Breech's life. A Detroit Lions' and Oakland Raiders' castoff, Breech visited Cincinnati during Thanksgiving week—and stayed, becoming the Bengals' all-time scoring leader with 1,151 points.

He was a perfect 9 for 9 in overtime field goals—an NFL record–kicked in two Super Bowls and just when he was about to be named the Most Valuable Player of Super Bowl XXIII, along came Joe Montana. The San Francisco 49ers pulled out a 20-16 victory at Joe Robbie Stadium in Miami on Montana's 10-yard TD pass to John Taylor with 34 seconds remaining—Taylor's only catch of the entire game.

A guy named Jerry Rice, with 11 catches for 215 yards and a TD, snatched the MVP trophy from Breech's grasp. "I was the MVP—for a while," Breech said. "After my 40-yard field goal (with 3:20 to go) put

When Breech kicked, he squeezed his normal size seven foot into a size five shoe, for the feel. He wanted nothing dragging on the turf.

us ahead, they took a preliminary ballot and 'Lap' (Bengals radio analyst Dave Lapham) said he asked 'em who won, and it was me. Obviously, the 49ers got the ball again. Rice won the MVP, and he said it was the best game he ever played."

Breech's story is a good one, but it gets a little complicated. Unable to stick with the Lions as their 8th-round draft pick in 1978, Breech kicked for the Raiders the entire 1979 season, but got released after the fourth preseason game in '80. The Bengals, ironically, had dumped Chris Bahr, their kicker for four years. Bahr got signed by Oakland.

"Raiders owner Al Davis had always been a big Chris Bahr fan, so when Bahr got released by the Bengals, I was concerned," Breech said. "Sure enough, they picked him up and released me. But the 13th week of 1980, I ended up in Cincinnati rather than Cleveland. I much preferred kicking on the AstroTurf in Cincinnati and not into that wind they have in Cleveland."

It was a turbulent year for kickers in Forrest Gregg's first season as Bengals' head coach. Ian Sunter lasted 10 games, making 11 of 20 field goals (55 percent). Then Sandro Vitiello missed his only two field goal attempts and was sent packing after two games. Enter Breech, who connected on 225 of 313 field goal attempts (71.9 percent) and 476 of 494 extra points over the course of 13 seasons.

His 13 straight field goals in 1990 is a club record that Doug Pelfrey tied in 1993 and '95. Breech was small in stature, but his right leg packed a punch. Why squeeze into a size 5 shoe when his normal shoe size was a 7?

"For feel," he said. "Just to get it real tight. I didn't want anything dragging on that turf."

Breech is known for his consistency, for coming through when the game was on the line. Like in the Super Bowl. "With three minutes to go, and you've got a 40-yard field goal, that to me is what it's all about in sports," Breech said. "To put you out there when it means something and see how you respond.

"Interestingly, I had a conversation with (NFL legend) Jan Stenerud during Super Bowl week and we talked about that. He said, 'Everything's going a hundred miles an hour. Just kind of slow everything down in your mind because it'll go normal.'

"My biggest thing was just getting the ball going in the right direction. I didn't care about killing it. I just wanted to get it going."

Losing the Super Bowl to the 49ers in 1982 hurt. Losing a second Super Bowl to San Francisco in 1989 hurt more. Reliving the disappointment

was brutal for Breech, who kicked in both games.

"To tell you the truth, it was such a privilege to have the opportunity to play in that game," Breech said. "But it leaves a little bitterness that we didn't quite pull one of them out and didn't have the opportunity to do a third. After you've already lost one, you really want to win that second opportunity. It's right there in your grasp. You're ahead. What more could you ask for? They've got 92 yards to go and three minutes to do it in.

"You've got some of the greatest players to ever play the game in Montana and Rice and that's probably why they *are* some of the greatest players. They rose to the occasion. That's what's sports is all about—putting it all on the line and see who rises to the occasion and pulls it out. And they did."

(Breech, 48, is a sales executive for The Hauser Group insurance firm in the Cincinnati suburb of Blue Ash. He's a voracious reader and plays golf.)

145

The Eraserman

¶Anthony Munoz, tackle (1980-'92)

The tears flowed on Monday, December 21, 1992, when Anthony Munoz announced his retirement to the team in an emotional farewell at the Bengals' Spinney Field training complex. Following the club's 20-10 victory over New England, he asked head coach Dave Shula if he could take a few minutes to address his teammates the next day. Permission granted. Everyone knew what was coming. The December 27 home game against Indianapolis would be his last hurrah.

"We went through the special teams film and a couple of other things before I got up there," Munoz said. "The whole time, I kept saying to myself, 'I'm going to be fine. I'm going to be fine. I'm going to get up there and I'm going to be able to talk and not be too emotional.' I had experienced a lot of memories here, and I thanked them for being a part of it. Then I lost it, and all of a sudden other guys were losing it."

Suddenly, quarterback Boomer Esiason and placekicker Jim Breech stood up. Doors opened. And the spoils of a fabulous career were hauled in for the victor. Esiason and Breech presented Munoz with a watch and a huge wall display containing a white No. 78 game jersey surrounded by 10 photos of Munoz in action. A plaque displayed these words: "Anthony Munoz 'The Best Ever' From The 1992 Bengals."

Munoz was finally at peace with his decision. He could relax and enjoy the crescendo of his final days in uniform. He was honored at a halftime ceremony and among the banners that adorned Riverfront Stadium, one near the Bengals locker room prophesied: "Munoz: Next Stop Canton."

We're talking about the greatest player in Bengals history here, so let's go back, all the way to New Year's Day 1980. Munoz had endured three knee surgeries in his college career. As a freshman, he tore ligaments in his right knee in the ninth game of the season. As a junior he tore ligaments in the same knee in the seventh game. Then, as a senior, he

"Generally," said Bengals' offensive line coach Jim McNally, "you just knew that if Anthony was playing, we'd erase his guy. We'd just call him The Eraserman."

For 13 years he played like he was trying to work his way into a starting slot.

—Max Montoya

147

tore ligaments in his left knee in the season opener.

"Each time I was hurt," Munoz said, "I felt bad because I couldn't play in the Rose Bowl. The last time, however, I knew I had the time to come back. No one believed me when I said I would be back for the bowl, but I knew I would be."

Someone who never doubted him was his wife, DeDe. "Anthony came home from the hospital and started jumping rope on one leg with the cast still on the other leg," she recalled. "He started lifting weights before the cast came off, and was running as soon as it came off."

Determined to make his final college game a special memory, Munoz dominated Ohio State's defensive line, cutting down a Buckeye defender with a devastating block that allowed tailback Charles White to score the winning touchdown in the Trojans' 17-16 come-from-behind victory.

"When he played in the Rose Bowl, my father and

brother Pete and I watched the game on television," Mike Brown said. "We just watched him. It got to be amusing because he toyed with the guy he was blocking. The three of us sat there and laughed out loud. The guy was so big and so good it was a joke. Our team doctor then, George Ballou, examined Anthony and told us he thought he was a reasonable risk. George gets some credit, too. We went forward with it and we were big winners."

Paul Brown dispatched his new head coach, Forrest Gregg, to USC for a personal workout. After rushing him a few times, Gregg, a Hall of Fame offensive tackle, decided to try a quick move to get past the young lineman. "I got tricky with him," Gregg said. "I rushed like I was going inside and then went outside on him. He reacted like a football player would. He jammed me on the chest with both hands and knocked me on my rear. He was very apologetic and I said, 'No, no, no, you did what you were supposed to do.' I thought, 'We've got to have this guy.'"

On April 29, 1980, the Bengals made him "their guy," selecting him with the third overall pick of the 1980 NFL Draft behind Oklahoma

tailback Billy Simms (Detroit) and Texas wide receiver Johnny "Lam" Jones (New York Jets). Mike Brown found out firsthand that Munoz was a determined negotiator. "He was from Los Angeles and somewhere I had seen the word burrito associated with him," Brown said. "I didn't know what a burrito was. That was before we had Mexican restaurants across the country. I assumed it was a small, determined donkey or something along those lines. Somehow I was quoted as saying something about him being a burrito."

Luckily for both parties, there were no hard feelings, and 72 hours after reporting to his first NFL training camp, Munoz became a starter. "I'd just been hired, so he didn't know me and I didn't know him," former Bengals offensive line coach Jim McNally said. "He started out on the second team, but after a while, it was apparent to everyone he was so dominant we had to move him up."

On a play in his first preseason game against Denver Broncos veteran defensive end Brison Manor, Munoz blocked him all the way over to the sidelines and off the field. "I had never seen a guy block anybody that far," McNally said. "He put him on a subway."

During his 13-year, 185-game career, Munoz received virtually every possible award. He was selected to 11 straight Pro Bowls (1981-'91) and named to the NFL's 75th Anniversary team. He was honored as the NFL Players Association Lineman of the Year in 1981, 1985, 1988, and 1989.

The NFL Alumni Association voted him the Offensive Lineman of the Year four times (1987, 1989-'91). Munoz's 1989 citation reads: "The NFL has three levels of offensive linemen. The bottom rung is for

Charles Steinbrunner (left) and Marty Williams

149

players aspiring to make the Pro Bowl. The next step is for those who have earned all-star status. Then there's Anthony Munoz. He's alone at the top." Munoz was such a talented athlete that he was utilized occasionally as a receiver. He caught seven passes on tackle-eligible plays, four resulting in touchdowns.

In 1998, in Canton, Munoz crossed the threshold to football immortality when he was inducted into the Pro Football Hall of Fame. As he stepped to the microphone to accept his coronation, the enormity of the moment finally hit him. He embraced his son, Michael, who gave the presentation speech, then grabbed the podium with outstretched arms, and took a deep breath in front of the crowd of 6,000.

He didn't lean on theatrics during his emotionally-charged, 12-minute oration. He told of a kid who grew up without a father, overcame three knee operations, and was drafted by the Bengals. He thanked his family, the Brown family, his coaches, and his mom, who, he said, gave him his work ethic. "You just go out and play and let your playing do the talking," he said. "Be competitive and be intense, but let people see your humility."

Mike Brown would say of Munoz, "The offensive linemen used to play softball on Mondays after the games. I would look out at Anthony, and the thing that caught my eye was he never moved like a big man. He moved like a little man, quick and nimble. He had unusual coordination.

"He lulled us to sleep. He was so good that we just thought playing left tackle was easy and never worried about it. When he left, we found out we should start worrying about it again. He was as good as they get."

His teammate, Dave Lapham, gave him the supreme accolade: "Anthony is not only a Hall of Fame football player, he's a Hall of Fame dad, friend, and community leader. He's as top-shelf as you can get. All the success he's had, it never affected him. He was always humble and polite. Even though he made 11 straight Pro Bowls, he was exactly the same. He never changed and that speaks volumes about the person."

(Munoz, 45, is in his seventh year as the analyst on the Bengals preseason TV network. He launched Integrity First Management with business partners in January, providing management services for pro athletes, and he and DeDe live in Mason. Their son, Michael, is a senior offensive tackle at Tennessee, and daughter, Michelle, is a junior forward on the Ohio State women's basketball team. Munoz is a spokesman for several companies, including Provident Bank, and is active with his foundation.)

We are protecting our QB with one of the best in the game. Anthony is the greatest offensive tackle the game has ever known.

—Sam Wyche

Charles Steinbrunner

151

Cadillac Cris

¶Cris Collinsworth, wide receiver (1981-'88)

College:
Florida
Hometown:
Titusville,
Florida
Height: 6-5,
Weight: 192
Pro Bowl: 3

You could knock him down, step on his face, and bloody his nose all over the place. Just remember this about Cris Collinsworth: He always, always, got up. "C.C." has that aw-shucks, Gomer-Pyle twang as one of the NFL's most popular broadcast analysts, and as a player, he had the physical build of actor Ray Bolger in *The Wizard of Oz*. He resembled a scarecrow without the straw. Opponents thought a stiff breeze would send him sprawling. They were wrong.

"My style? Not pretty, that's for sure," Collinsworth said. "I got a lot of sympathy votes from grandmothers who were afraid that somebody was going to destroy me, but that was part of my game, too. People always thought they could hurt me or hit me hard enough to knock me out of the game. My point was always to get up before they could get off the ground. No matter how hard they hit me, no matter how loopy I may have been, I was always trying to be up before they were because it sent a message back to them: 'Do whatever you want to do, but I'll be back.'

"Everybody has a chip on their shoulder about something, and I spent a lifetime of hearing people say: 'Ah, you're too skinny to play this game. You're going to get hurt.' Like a 5-6 point guard in the NBA, you're constantly trying to prove somebody wrong. So to me, being hurt or lying on the ground was an indication that somebody was being proven correct about me. My determination was never let anybody feel like they got me."

Collinsworth took plenty of punishment, but dished it out, too, with his spectacular play. Earning Pro Bowl honors in each of his first three seasons, he began and ended his career with trips to Super Bowl XVI and XXIII, and finished his eight-year NFL run with 417 catches for 6,698

Collinsworth was tougher than anyone thought, catching the ball over the middle and taking the hit. When the fans recalled his career, that's what they remembered.

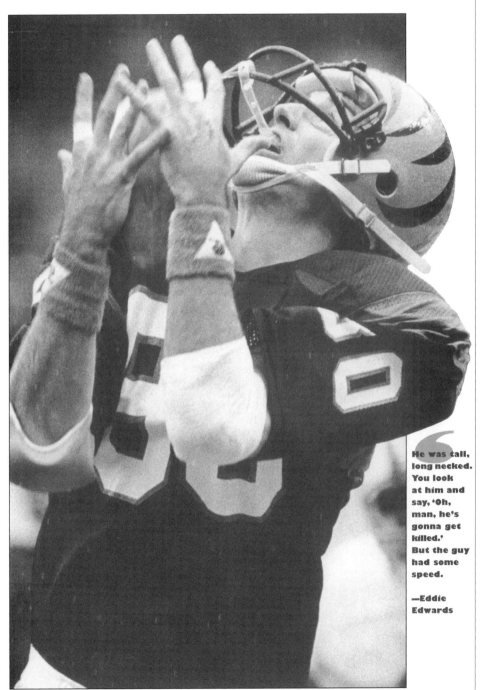

> He was tall, long necked. You look at him and say, 'Oh, man, he's gonna get killed.' But the guy had some speed.
>
> —Eddie Edwards

Bill Waugh

153

yards (a 16.1 average) and 36 touchdowns in 107 games.

His receptions rank second behind Carl Pickens (530) in club history and his yardage ranks third behind Issac Curtis (7,101) and Pickens (6,887). Yet for all of his accomplishments, including four 1,000-yard seasons, Collinsworth points to a game his rookie year that changed everything— a 41-21 victory at Cleveland on November 29, 1981. He caught five passes for 76 yards and two touchdowns, covering 39 and 7 yards, from quarterback Ken Anderson. That performance served as a springboard for his career by making him the subject of a *Sports Illustrated* cover story and was a notch in the Bengals' gun belt on their wild ride to the Super Bowl.

It made team founder Paul Brown proud, too, going back to his NFL roots and winning. "That one put me on the map," Collinsworth said. "That was the first time I really felt like, 'OK, I belong here. I can play this game.' It sort of marked we were for real on the NFL scene after a 6-10 year. For Paul Brown, that was something special. Every time we went back to Cleveland, he would have never said it publicly and he would have never been quoted as such, but you knew it meant a little something more to him."

A Lebanon, Ohio, native who was born at Miami Valley Hospital in Dayton, Collinsworth's family moved to Titusville, Florida, when he was four. His father, Lincoln "Abe" Collinsworth, wore uniform No. 10 on the University of Kentucky's 1958 NCAA Championship basketball team under head coach Adolph Rupp. As a freshman quarterback at the University of Florida, Cris stood in a line, trying on equipment, when a teammate got perturbed by the unusual amount of time it took Collinsworth to get fitted.

"They put about four helmets on my head. None of 'em fit," he said. "The guy who was next in line said: 'Will you hurry up, Collinsworth? Nobody's ever going to find a helmet to fit that big ol' Cadillac head of yours.' And it stuck. It sounds like a dream sort of nickname that nobody would ever get, something luxurious or speedy. But it really wasn't. It ended up being a great thing because usually when it was quoted, it was in a complimentary manner."

Collinsworth earned an accounting degree in 1981 at Florida, and a law degree in 1991 from the University of Cincinnati. But he learned that he didn't want to get stuck in an office or courtroom all day, and he focused on a broadcasting career, which has been nothing short of brilliant.

Outspoken, honest, and funny, Collinsworth has the uncanny ability

He'd take a big hit over the middle, get hit in the mouth, bleed, then get up and do it again. He wasn't the least bit apprehensive about throwing his head in there and blocking people. He was tough, man.

—Dave Lapham

155

to relate to armchair quarterbacks. He can also unleash prized one-liners. During Philadelphia's overtime victory over Green Bay in the 2003 postseason, Fox Sports cameras showed a man wearing a mask that had a football jammed in its mouth. "It's good to see Rush Limbaugh here," Collinsworth said.

He explained his quick wit this way: "I don't spend a lot of time between what comes to my mind and what comes out of my mouth," he said. "If I did, it would scare me to death. You just have to sort of react to what's going on and tell the truth. The hardest part about being a broadcaster is just telling the truth. It sounds silly, but if you don't, somebody else is going to be in there doing it in your place."

The best part? "My favorite part of the job is getting to watch great coaches and how many different ways there are to do the same exact thing, which is win football games," he said. "There is no single method to win games in the NFL. From Bill Walsh to Forrest Gregg to Joe Gibbs to Bill Parcells, they couldn't be any more different people, and yet each of those styles has been successful.

"As a broadcaster, you get inside that world that only players get to see. So I'm not only learning about football, but learning about leadership, running a business, and running a franchise. It's been a great education."

(Collinsworth, 45, is a two-time Emmy Award-winning NFL analyst for Fox Sports, a co-host on HBO's "Inside the NFL" and writes a column for NFL.com. He's also president of ProScan Imaging, a medical diagnostic imaging company in the Cincinnati area. He lives in Fort Thomas, Kentucky–"It's Mayberry," he said–and keeps busy with charity work, business investments, and his family: wife Holly and their four children. His favorite hobby? "I like to coach my kids.")

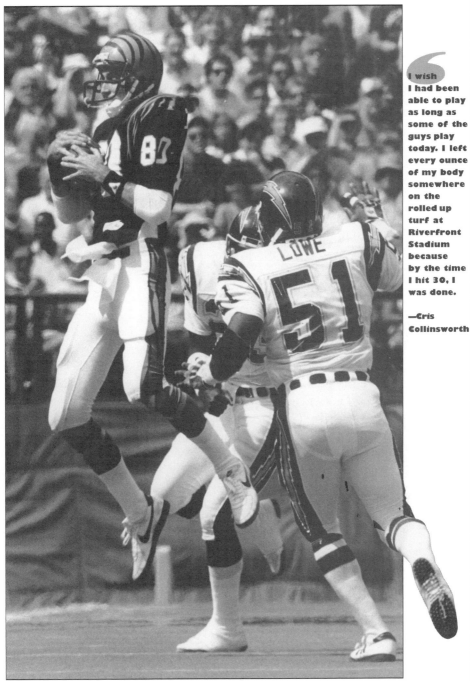

I wish I had been able to play as long as some of the guys play today. I left every ounce of my body somewhere on the rolled up turf at Riverfront Stadium because by the time I hit 30, I was done.

—Cris Collinsworth

Bill Waugh (left) and Charles Steinbrunner

157

The Big Stick

¶Forrest Gregg, head coach (1980-'83)

At 6-foot-4 and 250 pounds, Forrest Gregg was an imposing figure at offensive tackle for Vince Lombardi's juggernaut Green Bay Packers of the 1960s. And he was an intimidating presence in his first meeting with the Bengals players after being named head coach on December 28, 1979, at age 46. His piercing eyes were like lasers, burning holes in the souls of these talented but underachieving men who sat paralyzed with fear amid the funeral-home silence. This wasn't so much a wake-up call as it was culture shock. Suddenly, the players realized the party under Homer Rice was over.

"Forrest walks in and he was so pissed off," fullback Pete Johnson said. "He said, 'I'm going to tell you men one thing right now. If you think you can get somewhere by sticking your head up my ass, it ain't going to work. That's what's wrong with you guys. You don't know how to be a team. You don't care about each other. If there's a problem, you guys are going to solve it between yourselves. You go to the captains first. If they can't solve it, then you come to us.' "

Rice had a fertile mind but was too nice a guy to succeed as an NFL head coach. There was neither discipline nor accountability. Players ran roughshod over him. Rice's voice could be heard over the intercom begging guys to show up to meetings: "Wide receivers, you are now 10 minutes late for your meeting."

Under Gregg, the inmates would no longer be running the asylum. He demanded that his players show up on time, listen to the coaches, pay strict attention to detail, and play like hell. Gregg's motto was simply: Eight hours' work for eight hours' pay.

"The thing I most vividly remember," guard Dave Lapham said, "is him standing there, putting his hands on that podium, and I saw that Super Bowl ring. I thought, 'This guy played for Lombardi. Whatever he says, I'm going to listen.' He had instant credibility with me. He came on real strong. His whole message was: 'I'm going to be straight with you. You better not bullshit me.' "

"Forrest just was the greatest," said his fullback, Pete Johnson. "I put him in the Woody Hayes category. He was a real man."

158

Fellow guard Max Montoya remembers: "It was like night and day between him and Rice. Forrest came in with a big whip and a big stick. He probably didn't need one because he was an imposing figure anyway. He totally changed everybody's attitude."

In his book, *Run to Daylight*, Lombardi wrote, "Forrest Gregg is the finest player I ever coached." And Gregg returned the favor by saying Lombardi "made us realize that if the mind is willing, the body can."

Which is exactly the philosophy Gregg preached and the fuel he poured into the Bengals' psyche during his four-year reign when he generated a 34-27 record for the highest winning percentage (.557) among all nine head coaches in franchise history.

"That's the key, the team, and that's what you need to be," Gregg said from his home in Colorado Springs, Colorado. "We definitely had some talent. I can promise you that. I knew that when I coached in Cleveland playing against those guys. I definitely thought they were a good football team. But they had lost for a couple years and I just don't think they had much confidence in themselves.

"I wanted them to know that I believed in them and that I believed they were capable. The one way you do that is just be demanding of them. You say, 'Look, if you're the starting tackle, you're supposed to do the job. You're not supposed to get beat every play. You're not supposed to get beat at all. And if you're the quarterback, you're the coach on the field and you're supposed to do the job.' They believed that they were supposed to get the job done, and they did."

Gregg had a lot in common with Paul Brown, the Bengals' founder, owner, vice president and general manager. Both are Pro Football Hall of Famers. They are the only men to serve as head coach of both the Bengals and the Browns. Both were fired by ex-Browns boss Art Modell. All that made Gregg an ideal fit as Bengals head coach.

"I particularly knew how Paul felt because having been through there (Cleveland) myself and being fired was not any fun," Gregg said. "Paul was the guy who put the Browns together, who coached the team all those years, and they had all that success. And then for him to just have to walk away, I know it was extremely difficult. Nobody had to tell you that."

Four games stand out in Gregg's mind—a 27-24 loss to the Browns in the 1980 season finale at Riverfront Stadium; clinching the '81 AFC Central Division title with a 41-21 win at Cleveland; the Freezer Bowl; and the Super Bowl.

"In the final game of the season in 1980," Gregg said, "Cleveland had to win in order to go to the playoffs. I said to the players: 'Let's send 'em home for Christmas.' We battled back and forth in that ball game, and the thing I remember most is Pat McInally getting knocked out. I asked the doctors if he could play. They said, 'We think he'll be all right to play.' So I asked Pat and there was no question about what Pat was going to say, and he came back in and caught a TD pass. This team had nothing to gain from that ball game other than pride, and they played that game with pride. It was a heartbreaking loss, but it did something for us. It gave us the idea that, hey, we can play with anybody, and we can win."

Gregg played and coached in the two coldest games in NFL history—Green Bay's 21-17 Ice Bowl victory over the Dallas Cowboys for the NFL championship at Lambeau Field on December 31, 1967 (minus-13 degrees, minus-48 wind chill), and the Bengals' 27-7 Freezer Bowl victory over the San Diego Chargers for the AFC title at Riverfront Stadium on January 10, 1982 (minus-9 degrees, minus-59 wind chill).

So it's funny to hear Gregg say that he and his wife wanted to "beat the heat" by moving from Dallas to Colorado Springs. "I was colder in the Freezer Bowl because you're not playing," he said. "I'm glad I didn't have to handle the ball that day, and I admire those people who did."

And Bengals fans will always admire Gregg for leading them to the club's first Super Bowl. They won't forget Gregg's facial expressions—especially the bunny-rabbit twitch of his nose—and they won't forget that team's toughness, the embodiment of its coach.

"I just want them to remember we had a good football team and we played to the best of our ability every Sunday," Gregg said, "and that we respected the city, respected the fans, and did our very best not to let them down."

(Gregg, 70, lives in Colorado Springs, Colorado, with his wife Barbara. He still does public relations and consulting work for Bernie Glieberman, CEO of major developer Crosswinds Communities, which is headquartered in the Detroit suburb of Novi, Michigan. The Greggs have a daughter, Karen, who works in human resources for a company in Santa Fe, New Mexico, and a son, Forrest Jr., who works for Cincinnati Financial Corp. Gregg's favorite hobby is fly-fishing for trout with friends at private lakes some 45 minutes from his home).

The Machine

¶Rodney Holman, tight end (1982-'92)

Rodney Holman had just completed his sophomore year at Ypsilanti High School in 1976 when he got the opportunity to work a wrestling camp in Michigan that featured U.S. Olympic legend Dan Gable, who captured the freestyle gold medal at the 1972 Munich Games without surrendering a point to any of his opponents. "He was like a machine. He never stopped. He'd shoot for a single leg. I'd fight him off and then he'd go for the other leg. Right-left, right-left. I was exhausted. That proved to me right there, hey, you had to be in condition to press someone to the point where he made a mistake." Holman chuckled at the memory of being physically, mentally, and emotionally spent. It taught him a lesson he'd never forget: To make it in the NFL, you'd better be willing to give every ounce of effort, and when you think you have nothing left, give more.

College:
Tulane
Hometown:
Ypsilanti,
Michigan
Height: 6-3,
Weight:238
Pro Bowls: 3

Holman gave his all during a 14-year career that featured 11 seasons with the Bengals, including three Pro Bowls and three playoff trips, before moving on to the Detroit Lions. It was the little things, the extras, that helped Holman get an edge.

"I came in on Mondays and Anthony Munoz would be out there," he said. "We did extra running, then lifted weights. It paid off in the fourth quarter and it paid off after the halfway mark of the season when other teams were winding down. We'd be making a playoff push and conditioning played a big part. We came up with that innovative no-huddle offense, so you had to be somewhat like a machine to handle it."

Holman played 213 NFL games, second in league history for a tight end behind Pete Metzelaars (235). His 318 catches as a Bengal rank sixth on the club's career list—first among tight ends—and he stands eighth all-time in Bengals receiving yards with 4,329 to go with 34 Bengals touchdowns. For his career, he caught 365 passes for 4,771 yards (a 13.1-yard average) and 36 TDs.

Holman was the quintessential tight end, a complete football package who could block defensive ends and linebackers.

I figured they were going to punish me if I caught the ball, so I tried to give a little bit back. It's a physical game.

—Rodney Holman

163

"I tried to be the complete package," he said. "There were guys way ahead of me like Hall of Famer John Mackey who were all-around tight ends. They didn't come out of the game. They went in and blocked the defensive ends and outside linebackers. But that style is becoming extinct. Nowadays, they don't even expect the tight end to block a defensive end."

"In a football sense, he was all business," said Sam Wyche. "If there was something he didn't understand, he'd work with it until he did. He was one of those guys who had to be totally off-duty before he lightened up."

Fellow tight end Jim Riggs cited him for his knowledge of defenses. "When we were watching film of the other team, he was the first one to call out the defenses. He knew what he could do even when things got real complicated." And Boomer Esaison said, "I'm not sure there was a better tight end in football."

A quiet guy, Holman simply let his play speak for him, such as his 10-catch, 161-yard performance on October 7, 1990, when the Bengals beat the Los Angeles Rams in overtime, 34-31, on the road—his most memorable game. "I was never a 'me' guy," he said. "We had a great arsenal of receivers. I forced myself to play well because it gave me a chance to stay on the field more."

In 1982, the Bengals made him a third-round draft pick (82nd overall) out of Tulane. He came highly recommended from offensive coordinator Lindy Infante, a former assistant for the Green Wave. The Bengals had outstanding wide receivers in Issac Curtis and Cris Collinsworth, Tim McGee, and Eddie Brown, but right there with them was Holman, who emerged as a brilliant blocker and tough, disciplined, physical, sure-handed receiver—the complete tight end.

"Paul Brown loved him," said Dr. D.S. Ping, Holman's agent in Saline, Michigan. "But when I was negotiating that first contract with them, Mike Brown got irritated with me. He said, 'You make it sound like this kid is an All-Pro.' I told him, 'Rodney is not just a guy. His talent is unmeasurable.' As it turned out, the proof was in the pudding."

And just think. The springboard was a wrestling mat in a Michigan gym with Holman getting twisted like a pretzel at the hands of an Olympic champion.

(Holman, 44, is retired and living in Slidell, Louisiana, 25 miles east of New Orleans, where he hunts and fishes. He was an assistant for the New Orleans Saints (1998-'99) and the Bengals. His goal is to get back into coaching in the NFL.)

> " I was a team player. I didn't seek the limelight. I played it hard, played it well, and gave it all I had.
>
> —Rodney Holman

Bill Waugh

165

Tough Guy

¶*Tim Krumrie, defensive tackle (1983-'94)*

Standing on the gas of his Harley-Davidson, in a T-shirt, blue jeans, and ostrich-skin boots, Tim Krumrie is in heaven. Butting heads with him in the football trenches, however, was hell. That's where All-America center Dave Rimington found himself in the summer of 1983 at Wilmington College. Rookie combatants in head coach Forrest Gregg's "Nutcracker Drill"—in which a defensive lineman takes on a block from an offensive lineman, with a running back bursting off tackle—Krumrie forgot he was a 10th-round draft pick, the 276th player chosen, and kicked the tail of the draft's 25th overall selection.

College: Wisconsin
Hometown: Mondovi, Wisconsin
Height: 6-2, Weight:274
Pro Bowls: 2

"Rimington was the No. 1 draft choice and had some pretty high credentials coming into our training camp, and Tim was a lowly-round draft choice who wasn't given a prayer to make our football team," linebacker Jim LeClair said.

"But yet he probably did the most in establishing himself as a player that day. Krumrie just manhandled Rimington. He got an ovation from everybody that was watching. That was probably the biggest thing he has ever done in his career to make sure he made that team."

The players hated the drill, which was designed to toughen them up, but they all gathered 'round to watch Krumrie's exhibition. He had been a heavyweight wrestling star in college, and reported to camp at 250 pounds.

Rimington checked in at 292. Guard Dave Lapham remembers the incident well, how Krumrie—with his Incredible Hulk strength and leverage —stripped the luster off Rimington's star status, reducing the two-time Outland Trophy winner to ordinary.

"Forrest initially had Rimington paired up with somebody else," Lapham said. "But Krumrie just jumped right in there and kicked his ass. Then Timmy jumped up and screamed at him and spit and said, 'I'm going to be your worst nightmare every f—— snap of your career!' They went at it again and Krumrie kicked his ass again. It was unbelievable."

At right: The original tough man. "I thrive on exhaustion and inflicted pain," he said once. "I take myself over the edge."

166

It was also a sign of things to come. Krumrie, whose reputation for toughness is unmatched in club history, never missed a game in his 12-year career, even after his left leg shattered in the Super Bowl.

He started 166 of 193 games and had a streak of 160 starts in 161 games. He led the Bengals in tackles five times, unheard of for an interior lineman, and was selected as a Pro Bowl starter after the '87 and '88 seasons.

Asked once to define a Krumrie player, Tim smiled and said: "High energy. No matter what the odds, what the score, I'll fight you every step of the way."

Every Bengals fan remembers the horrifying leg injury Krumrie suffered at the height of his career in Super Bowl XXIII on January 22, 1989, at Joe Robbie Stadium in Miami. It occurred on the first play of San Francisco's second possession with the 49ers pinned on their 3-yard line after a 36-yard Lee Johnson punt.

Krumrie, a nose tackle who had 152 tackles to lead the Bengals for the fourth straight year, was pursuing running back Roger Craig on a trap play. As he turned sharply to his left, his left cleat got caught in the soft

Said one writer: "If ever a man were put on this earth to do one thing, it is Tim Krumrie, plugging the middle of the defensive line like a dump truck in an alley."

"There was no neutral, no second gear for him. It was either all-out or nothing. He was just a psycho.
—*Dave Lapham*

Bill Waugh

169

grass and his left leg twisted and snapped, resulting in a broken tibia and fibula.

"I heard it snap," Krumrie told *The Miami Herald*. "It's rough. This is the first injury I've ever had. But at least it won't need reconstruction. Give me 10 weeks and I'll be back."

Wheeled off on a stretcher with his leg in an air cast, Krumrie sipped a beer and watched the first three quarters on a portable TV in the locker room. He refused to leave the stadium until the start of the fourth quarter. Finally, he was taken to Mercy Hospital.

"I came with the guys. I wanted to leave with the guys," Krumrie had said. "But the coaches and doctors told me they could take better care of me here."

A nurse at Mercy said admitting Krumrie was difficult: "He was very pleasant but very intense and into the game. I was trying to interview him, but he was watching the game. He was very apologetic."

Krumrie was right, you know. He fought back from the injury and was in the lineup for the '89 opener. In rehab, he lifted so much weight, he broke off a couple of the screws holding his leg together. Playing with a metal rod in his leg, he recorded 73 tackles (45 solos), three sacks, and a fumble recovery that comeback season.

There were times after games when Krumrie—his cut-off sleeves showing those thick, ironworker arms—would stand at his Riverfront Stadium dressing stall and let the blood ooze from the patch of scar tissue that had split open on the bridge of his nose.

As *Dayton Daily News* feature columnist Tom Archdeacon wrote: "He didn't get that cauliflowered left ear, the scarred chin and those steel pins in his knee from Emily Post politeness. The toughest Bengal has a metal rod in his left leg, meaty fingers that are as bent and gnarled as driftwood, and a bobbed, swollen nose that looks as if it has been reworked with a hammer. Yet with all those souvenirs, he never missed a game. He played with wrenched knees, internal bleeding and once pulled a hamstring on Thursday and played on Sunday."

Even now, as a coach, Krumrie is a cult hero to fans. They still approach him with adoration for his blue-collar work ethic. "You come into the league," he said, "and it's like, 'What do you want to be remembered as?' I always wanted to be remembered as a good football player and sometimes I look back and say, 'I'm the guy who

Krumrie in form, during the AFC Championship win, 21-10 over Buffalo in January of 1989 at Riverfront Stadium.

broke his leg in the Super Bowl.' But probably the biggest thing is, no matter who you see, everybody says, 'You played your ass off all the time.' There's a guy who came out to practice and said, 'Tim, I really liked the way you played football.' Just out of the blue. I didn't have a clue who he was. That kind of makes you feel good that they still remember."

(Krumrie, 44, is in his second season as defensive line coach of the Buffalo Bills. His 20-year relationship with the Bengals—12 as a player and eight as an assistant coach—ended in 2002, with head coach Dick LeBeau's firing. Krumrie's hobbies include lifting weights, riding his motorcycles, and taking care of his quarter horses.)

Little Big Man

¶James Brooks, tailback (1984-'91)

James Brooks is the poster child for everything that's right and wrong with college and professional sports. One day you're making a king's ransom for playing a kid's game. Then, suddenly, your name appears in agate type under "transactions" in the sports section, your career is over and your life goes to hell.

College:
Auburn
Hometown:
Warner Robins,
Georgia
Height: 5-10
Weight: 180
Pro Bowls: 4

Brooks could run—he gained 7,962 rushing yards, 3,621 receiving yards, and scored 79 TDs during a brilliant 12-year, 162-game career for four teams—but he couldn't hide from his personal problems and got sent to jail, a sad, sour ending to a sweet career.

On the field, Brooks was the complete tailback, a quicksilver player who darted through openings at the line of scrimmage, dashed around defenders, caught seemingly every pass thrown his way and stuck his facemask into the shoulder pads of linebackers and defensive ends in pass protection.

The owner of a supreme football work ethic, Brooks went to Houston every year before training camp to work out in the intense heat and humidity with a track coach, so that he wouldn't wilt at Wilmington College. "I push myself hard," Brooks said in 1990, "so I know no one can push me as hard as I've already pushed myself."

The payoff was a trip to four Pro Bowls after seasons in which his rushing total reached 1,087 yards (1986), 931

Brooks, said one sportswriter, "has thrown his 180-pound body around the arena for a decade and still looks like a new penny."

172

I love the pain. Say what you want about me. You can't say I'm not tough enough.

—James Brooks

Bill Waugh

173

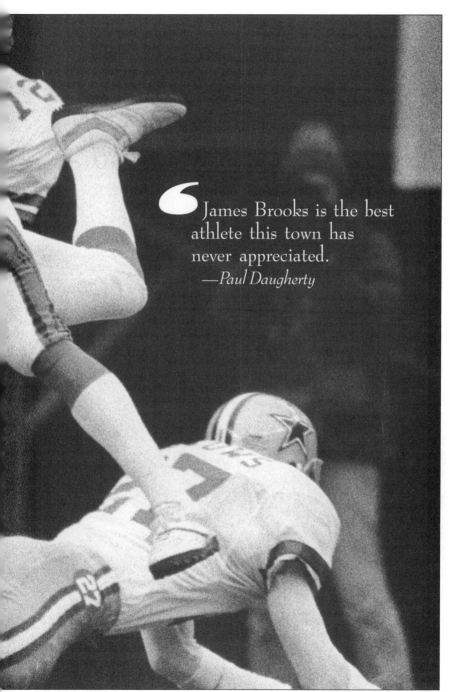

'James Brooks is the best athlete this town has never appreciated.
—*Paul Daugherty*

Bill Waugh

175

Bill Waugh

176

(1988), 1,239 (1989) and 1,004 (1990); a Super Bowl following the '88 season; and league-wide respect.

"He was a shifty, make-you-miss back, the kind of guy who had quick, instant acceleration," Bengals' running backs coach Jim Anderson said. "Pound for pound, he was probably one of the toughest guys who ever played the position.

"As soon as the season was over, he'd take a couple weeks off but then he would prepare himself for the next season by working on his physical condition, his stamina, his durability. The only thing that would stop him is a broken bone, and he'd get that taped up and come back and play."

The greatest trade in club history came on May 29, 1984, when the Bengals acquired Brooks from the San Diego Chargers in a straight-up deal for fullback Pete Johnson. "Pete was at the end of his career and JB was just starting to peak," Dave Lapham said. "You know how big surprises come in small packages? That was Brooks. He had no fear about running guys over. They'd come up to make a hit on him. They'd set up soft, waiting for his moves and he'd dump 'em. And he could make moves on 'em. He was the total package."

Brooks said all the talent that surrounded him "is making the span of my football life longer." He thought he could play forever. Fast forward to November of 1999. Brooks stands in a Cincinnati courtroom, wearing a pale blue jumpsuit issued by the Hamilton County Justice Center. And a judge sends him back to jail for three months for failing to pay more than $110,000 in child support.

"I played football and I done well," Brooks, the Bengals' career rushing leader at the time with 6,447 yards, told the judge. "But at some time, I lost all that I had." Brooks' attorney described his client as a broke, unskilled laborer who earned $7 an hour at a warehouse job before moving to England in 1996; who got by for most of his life because he could play football; who struggled to find his place in society after his career ended in 1992 after short stints with Cleveland and Tampa Bay; who "suffered the indignities of a man who has fallen from great heights."

The judge asked Brooks how he got through Auburn University without learning how to read. "I didn't have to go to class," he said. Brooks was ordered to stay in Cincinnati for his five-year probation, get a job so he could start supporting his kids and to take literacy classes.

(Brooks, 46, chose not to be interviewed for this book. Jim Anderson said Brooks is employed in Cincinnati and is working hard to get his life together. "There's no question about that," Anderson said.)

The Blond Bomber

¶Boomer Esiason, quarterback (1984-'92,'97)

College: Maryland
Hometown: Manhasset, New York
Height: 6-5
Weight:224
Pro Bowls: 4

Boomer Esiason dropped back, threw the ball, collided with Cleveland Browns defensive tackle Bob Golic, then cut a deal with his friendly enemy. It was November 10, 1985, a Bengals' 27-10 victory in Cincinnati. "As he threw the ball, I hit him," Golic said. "I heard this moan and this big gust of air come out of his lungs, which is always a great feeling for us defensive guys. I looked up and said, 'Boomer, you OK?' He's lying there and he says, 'Yeah, I'm fine. Hey, Bob, I've got to talk to you about something.'

"He had completed the pass and the play was going on. Somebody's chasing this guy who caught the ball. Boomer goes: 'I've got a buddy up in Cleveland who opened a boot company. He's got a couple stores. He wanted to know if you could sign a couple of pictures for him, and he'll give you a free pair of boots.'

"I said: 'Yeah, sure, I'd be glad to.' After the game, we're standing face to face on the field. A couple of my buddies were at the game and said, 'Were you fighting with Boomer?' I said, 'No, he was giving me the phone number of the guy's secretary to give her a call so I could find out where to send the pictures.' "

Fast forward to November 24, 1985, a 24-6 Browns' victory in Cleveland. "Early in the game, Boomer drops the ball," Golic added. "There's this huge pile. I see Boomer down at the bottom.

I'm trying to pull the ball out and I'm yelling, 'Give me the ball, Boomer, give me the ball.'

"He looks up through these legs and arms and goes, 'Hey, Bob, did you ever get a hold of that guy about those boots?' At which point, the other veterans are saying, 'Hey, Boomer, can I get some boots, too?' "

Esiason laughs at the memory. "All I remember is seeing his ugly face, his big, hairy beard, and his stinky breath. I'm like, 'Man, I've got the ball, just leave it alone. Oh, by the way, did you get your boots?' "

Teammates called Esiason the greatest leader they've ever seen. As Golic's story suggests, Boomer could

"What is amazing is the pounding quarterbacks take in this league," said QB coach Dana Bible. "And they don't come any tougher than Boomer."

I love being a QB. The QB is like the real live American hero. It's the crème de la crème in all of sports. Everybody wants to be the QB.

—Boomer Esiason

179

even lead opponents, too. He threw for at least 3,000 yards six straight years (1985-90), won the NFL Most Valuable Player award in the Super Bowl season of 1988, and his 27,149 passing yards ranks second to Ken Anderson (32,838) in club history. But Esiason played six fewer seasons in Cincinnati than Anderson.

"I was always a very aggressive player," the famous No. 7 said. "I was aggressive in the meeting rooms. I was aggressive on the practice field. And I aggressively approached the game on the field mentally. I could run if I had to, but I always considered myself a drop-back, in-the-pocket, play-action quarterback.

"I try to explain this to people and they have a hard time understanding it. There had to be a commitment by all of us, including the coaches,

"In Cincinnati," said sportswriter Lonnie Wheeler, "Boomer Esiason is proof that God acknowledges football..."

to accentuate something the whole team did well. I've often said the quarterback gets too much credit when things are going well, and too much blame when things aren't going so well."

Born Norman Julius Esiason on April 17, 1961, he kicked so hard during his mother's pregnancy that his nickname was a natural. Mrs. Irene Esiason died of cancer when Boomer was 5, leaving his father and two older sisters to dote on him. Mr. Norman Esiason, a safety engineer in New York City, died of a massive coronary on Thanksgiving night, 1999, at the age of 77.

"Boomer truly had the greatest father you could have to be a star athlete," said Jerrold Colton, Esiason's longtime agent. "His father just supported and backed him in everything. He

made every practice, every game, and never interfered. His father just poured everything into him. He always told him, 'Son, you can do anything you want to in this world.'

"He would ask his father things like, 'Really, dad, you think I can be an NFL player?' He would say, 'Absolutely.' He instilled in him that confidence. That's what makes him. And as soon as he did make it, he kept telling him, 'Never forget where you came from.' He'd constantly hit him over the head with that."

Upset at falling into the second-round pick (38th overall) of the 1984 NFL Draft, Esiason came to Cincinnati with a chip on his shoulder. But he won over fans and teammates as a rookie by throwing the game-tying TD pass to Anthony Munoz on a tackle-eligible play in the Bengals' 20-17 overtime win at Cleveland.

The transition from the low-key Anderson to Esiason's dynamic personality and high-octane arm in 1985 wasn't easy. "Boomer was a guy who believed in his own ability beyond what any of us believed when he first walked in the door," wide receiver Cris Collinsworth said. "I remember Steve Kreider saying, 'If that guy ever gets to play quarterback, I'm going home.' Just catching it without anybody around was hard because it was a rocket shot.

"But he had something that went beyond the game. He had a charisma, a leadership style that you kind of read about in the books. Sort of confidence bordering on arrogance, but it really worked. He had a great sense of humor to go along with it. He would point to (Buffalo Bills defensive end) Bruce Smith and tell him that Anthony Munoz was getting ready to whip his tail. Anthony would look at him and say, 'Would you please shut up. I've got a hard enough job down here today.' That's the kind of stuff that legends are made from."

Esiason's greatest statistical game finished off the darkest week in franchise history. Head coach Sam Wyche had barred a female reporter from the locker room after the Bengals' 31-16 loss at Seattle in a Monday night game on October 1, 1990, that led to a $27,941 fine by the NFL. The team stayed on the West Coast afterward because it faced the Los Angeles Rams on October 7. Three days after the Monday nighter came the famous "Victoria C" scandal in which 12 Bengals were accused of raping a woman in a suburban Seattle hotel room. No criminal charges were filed against any of the players, but the case wasn't settled until April 1993.

At his best, Boomer is the Fourth of July.

—Paul Daugherty

"It was extremely memorable because of all the things that were focused around the team," Esiason said. "By the time we get off the bus in L.A., you're talking about one of the most bizarre—if not the most bizarre—weeks in the history of the Bengals."

Amidst all the chaos, Esiason threw for a franchise record 490 yards, including three TDs, in the 34-31 overtime victory that ended on Jim Breech's 44-yard field goal at the 3:04 mark in OT.

"What I remember most about that game is that I had to take a piss in the worst way in the fourth quarter," Esiason said. "When it went into overtime, I just remember my bladder getting ready to explode. Finally, Jim Breech kicked the winning field goal and I couldn't wait to go to the bathroom. The interesting thing was every female reporter known to mankind was in our locker room. I told 'em I had to go to the bathroom before I could give an interview."

But Esiason saved some of his best for last. Returning to Cincinnati in 1997 as a backup after stints with the New York Jets (1993-'95) and Arizona Cardinals (1996), he took over

Dave Lapham once said that if Boomer had Ken Anderson's accuracy, he would have set records no one could ever touch.

Skip Peterson

for an ineffective Jeff Blake and engineered a 4-1 finish to a 7-9 season, then retired at age 36.

"I left on top of my game," he said, "with my kids feeling the positive aspects of being a professional quarterback. They didn't hear the boos. They didn't see the (1987) strike year. They didn't see the 3-13 year in New York. They only saw the positive. That was a very powerful thing for me, to leave knowing that I played some of the best football of my career, and that I would not have the anxiety associated with what comes along with really caring about your craft."

Team president Mike Brown offered him a two-year contract worth $8 million if he reached all his incentives, but Esiason turned it down. The pull of his family and the opportunity to join the telecast of ABC's Monday Night Football games sealed the deal.

"I sat in Mike Brown's office and I was very honest with him," Esiason said. "It was so powerful and so strong and it was so good. I said to him: 'I don't know if I can give you 16 games at that level.' I can't tell you how powerful those final days were for me and how significant they were because of what it meant to my kids. It was probably one of reasons Mike thought it would be good for me to go to ABC. I respected Mike for his honesty back then. I think he respected me as well."

(Esiason, 43, is the nation's leading figure in the fight against Cystic Fibrosis. Esiason's son, Gunnar, was diagnosed with the disease in 1993, and since then the Boomer Esiason Foundation has generated more than $35 million toward research in finding a cure and helping patients and their families enjoy better lives. "We put a real face and a name to the disease, which is what I'm most proud of," he said. Esiason and his family—wife Cheryl, Gunnar and daughter Sydney—live on Long Island. He is a co-host for CBS-TV's "NFL Today" show; is the analyst for Monday Night Football games on CBS Radio Sports/Westwood One; hosts a nationally-syndicated radio show called "In the Huddle"; does projects for WLW-AM (700) in Cincinnati; and writes for NFL.com. He took up ice hockey at age 39. Golf and traveling are his other hobbies.)

Boomer: "If somebody said, 'What do I do on a play, I would know everything about his job on that play—the linemen's steps, the blocking technique. If they couldn't communicate the calls, I communicated the calls for them. I'd take them out to dinner, have them over for parties, and travel with them. I made sure everybody understood that I knew I was not the most important person."

My last touchdown pass was *77* yards. My dad died at *77*. He died on November *25*. Two plus five. Seven.

—Boomer Esiason

Bill Garlow

185

A Beautiful Mind

¶Sam Wyche, head coach (1984-'91)

The beginning was beautiful. The ending was ugly. Inbetween, head coach Sam Wyche—former Bengals quarterback—took us on a roller coaster ride of highest highs and lowest lows. His team soared into the Super Bowl after the 1988 season only to bottom out in 1991 when a once star-studded roster became depleted by free-agent defections, leading to his dismissal after eight turbulent years. And just to clarify, Wyche didn't resign. He was fired by Bengals president Mike Brown on December 23, 1981, the day after a 29-7 victory over New England ended a 3-13 season that was marred by the August 5 death of team founder Paul Brown.

More on Wyche's D-Day later. For now, he's the Buffalo Bills' new quarterbacks coach, having overcome a tragedy in 2000 when a doctor, attempting to biopsy Wyche's lymph nodes, accidentally cut the nerve to Wyche's left vocal chord. The biopsy was negative, yet Wyche's blossoming TV broadcasting career was suddenly over. Now that his voice has improved, he's back on the field, where life is wicky, wacky, and wonderful.

The birth certificate of this offensive genius, no-huddle mastermind, skilled communicator, and deep thinker reads Samuel David Wyche, but his middle name should have been "Controversy" because he thrived on it. He could never just watch gasoline spill. He always had to throw a match on it. He had running feuds with head coaches Chuck Noll of Pittsburgh and Jerry Glanville of Houston. He got fined for refusing *USA Today* female reporter Denise Tom locker-room access after a 31-16 loss to Seattle at the Kingdome on Oct. 1, 1990. And he was crucified for his famous "golf to be played and tennis to be served" speech—saying too much emphasis is placed on wins and losses—after a 14-13 loss in Cleveland in 1991.

All that pales to the events of December 10, 1989, at Riverfront Stadium in a 24-17 loss to Seattle. With 10 minutes remaining and the Seahawks backed up at their 4-yard

"Wyche wanted to coach the world," said sportswriter Paul Daugherty, "and, generally, he considered himself up to the task."

Paul Brown kept Wyche's playbook from 1969, then gave it to Wyche after hiring him as head coach in 1984. "He had everything in order," PB said. "He was a student of the game. He was special."

187

line, fans at the south end began pelting the field with snowballs. When the Seahawks refused to snap the ball because of the snowballs, the officials stopped play.

Wyche ran across the field to the Seattle sideline, grabbed the public address microphone, and screamed the most memorable words in franchise history: "Will the next person that sees ANYBODY throw anything onto this field, point 'em out. We'll get 'em out of here. YOU DON'T LIVE IN CLEVELAND! YOU LIVE IN CINCINNATI!" The crowd of 54,744 went bonkers.

In Indianapolis during a break from the 2004 NFL Combine, Wyche recalled the incident. "When the snowball throwing started, I went over to the referee and he wanted it stopped, too," Wyche said. "I told him: 'If you'll let me say something on the microphone, I'll stop this.' I had no idea what I was going to say. I just said what was on my mind and the place went berserk."

Of course, Browns fans were irate. So to mend fences in the offseason, Wyche traveled to Cleveland, sat in a carnival-style dunking booth, and raised $11,000 for the Salvation Army's Family Crisis Center. Browns quarterback Bernie Kosar and his father helped Wyche construct the booth, and fans paid to throw big rawhide dog bones to trigger the latch that would dunk Wyche. Kosar was the first contestant. It took him five throws to get Wyche in the water.

"It takes an awfully big man to come into town and raise money for charity," Kosar said. "I wanted Cleveland fans to know it wasn't hatred," Wyche said, "just competitiveness. We happened to sweep them that year. My one great line, nobody laughed at. Sitting in the booth, I said: 'Ye without a win cast the first bone.' There was dead silence."

Wyche—given the "Wicky Wacky" nickname in 1987 by Steelers' assistant coach Dick Hoak—once extended his hand to Noll after a game and Noll declined to shake it. He feuded with Glanville because he didn't like the Oilers' over-aggressive style of play.

So he ran up the score whenever possible. The Bengals' 54-point victory margin in a 61-7 win over the visiting Oilers on December 17, 1989, remains the largest in team history. And their most recent playoff victory came over the Oilers, 41-14, on January 6, 1991, at Riverfront Stadium. Cincinnati led 20-0 at halftime. It wasn't enough.

"Sam comes in at halftime and he's tippin' over water buckets," safety Solomon Wilcots said. "I'm telling you right then and there he would have made Forrest Gregg look like a choir boy. 'I'll fine anybody who lets up in the second half! I want 30 more points on this God-damn team!' He hated

Jerry Glanville. Sam was nice and cool and giddy, but he could go crazy."

Before he was fired, Wyche asked Brown if the coaches' end-of-the-year meeting with management could be delayed a week because the season was so draining. "Mike wanted to have that meeting on Monday, the day after the season," Wyche said. "This time, the other coaches weren't in there. It was just me. Katie was taking notes. Mike was at the other end of the table and Pete was on my left.

"During the course of the conversation, Mike said, 'I don't want you to elaborate and talk so much at press conferences after the games. Just tone everything down.' I said, 'Mike you've been around me for eight years. This is me. That's just my style.'

"He read some sample answers that he would like for me to do. 'It was a good game. The guys played hard. We'll be ready next week.' My answer was, 'Mike, I don't know if I can do that or not. That's just not me. I'll try, but I can't promise you I'll do that. That's not my nature.'

"That's when he leaned over and said, 'You just resigned.' I thought he was kidding. Mike and I, to this day, are good friends, socially and professionally. I raised my hand and said, 'Hey, wait a second, isn't that my line? Don't I get to say that?' He said, 'You just resigned.' I realized he was serious.

"I reached over and shook Pete and Katie's hand, reached across the table and shook his hand. I was starting to go into shock at that point. The funny part was, I must have looked back to say goodbye as I was reaching for the door knob. I missed the knob. (Business manager) John Murdough happened to be in the hall.

"He saw the expression on my face. He said, 'I knew it. I knew something was wrong.' We walked down the hall and as we passed each secretary, they started tearing up because they could tell something had happened. I just went out the back door. That was it."

(Wyche, 59, was hired as quarterbacks coach of the Buffalo Bills in February, ending an eight-year hiatus from the NFL. He compiled records of 64-68 (.485) with the Bengals from 1984-'91, and 23-41 (.359) with Tampa Bay from 1992-'95. His offseason home is Pickens, S.C., where he lives with wife Jane. The couple has two children, Zak and Kerry, and two grandchildren. He's a member of the All American Speakers bureau, commanding $20,000 to $30,000 per speech. He is an accomplished magician and airplane pilot, and plays golf, tennis, and the guitar.)

He was the most unique, innovative, thought-provoking coach in the history of the NFL. The most enjoyable, unique moments I ever had as a football player were when he was my coach. When they took him away and brought in Dana Bible, I wanted to slit my wrists.

—Boomer Esiason

189

The Coach on the Field

¶Bruce Kozerski (1984-'95)

Bruce Kozerski was fiery, upbeat, positive and intense, a guy who brought enthusiasm to the field not just on Sundays, but every day. He spent his entire 12-year career in Cincinnati, playing center, guard and tackle, and was a leader on an offensive line that clawed its way to a franchise-best 12-4 record and 8-0 home mark in 1988, a season that culminated with a trip to Super Bowl XXIII in Miami.

College:
Holy Cross
Hometown:
Wilkes-Barre,
Pennsylvania
Height: 6-4,
Weight: 287

"I wasn't the strongest guy in the world, but I was quick and smart," Kozerski said. "I spent all week long working on my game plan within the game plan. It depended on who I played. When you go against the same guy like (Cleveland defensive tackle) Bob Golic twice a year, he knows me as well as I know him. So you have to play games with your footwork and technique because, if you don't, he'll take advantage of it.

"You have to occasionally change your technique and do some different things. Same thing with your pass blocking. The goal was to take away what the guy did best, take away his top one or two moves and make him fall back on his third or fourth move."

Most guys have difficulty mastering one job. Well, "Koz" played four positions in the same game—a 16-12 Bengals' victory at Pittsburgh on December 2, 1990. He started at center, moved to left guard, then to right guard, and finally to right tackle when Joe Walter went down.

And let's not forget he was the club's long-snapper. Talk about a tight-knit unit. The offensive line in that glory-filled '88 season—with Kozerski at center, Bruce Reimers at left guard and Max Montoya at right guard, Hall of Famer Anthony Munoz at left tackle and Walter at right tackle—was inseparable. And it included

Kozerski was a physics major in college and the antithesis of the monosyllabic pro jock. An offensive linchpin, he played his entire career in Cincinnati.

190

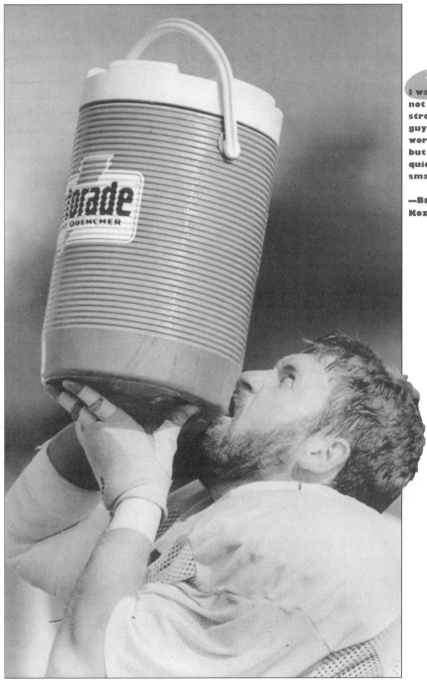

> **I was not the strongest guy in the world, but I was quick and smart.**
>
> —Bruce Kozerski

quarterback Boomer Esiason.

"We just all got together like family," Kozerski said. "I'd fight with my brothers more than I'd fight with those guys. The thing with that group was, all you had to do was your job. You were playing with guys up front that you knew and trusted. And you knew the guy playing behind you was as good as there was.

"Boomer was an honorary offensive lineman. He just had that confidence. Periodically, he'd get in your face and say, 'That's the second time that guy's hit me in this series. Pick it up.' He was not afraid to look you in the eye and say, 'Let's get it going. That's unacceptable.'"

Kozerski played in 172 games with 137 starts. Not bad for a ninth-round draft pick from Holy Cross in Worcester, Massachusetts. His last start turned out to be his last game—October 29, 1995, against visiting Cleveland. It was Game 8 that year. One of the Browns' defensive tackles got caught off balance and center Darrick Brilz threw him down. Instead of landing on the AstroTurf, the Cleveland player crashed into Kozerski's right leg, breaking it.

"It was nothing intentional," Kozerski said. "It's something anybody would have done. He just happened to land on the back of my right leg."

The dean of the Bengals' roster at the time, Kozerski could've tied Munoz for the most years played by a Bengals offensive lineman (13) in '96, but he decided to retire before the season.

The anti-big-dumb-jock who earned a bachelor's degree as a physics major, carrying a 3.7 GPA, Kozerski made a living banging heads for 12 years and was able to walk away with all his marbles, and some wonderful memories.

"I'll never forget the AFC Championship game (a 21-10 victory) against Buffalo," Kozerski said. "Probably for 20 minutes after the game, nobody left. The fans were standing and cheering, and I didn't want to leave the field. The Super Bowl after that was phenomenal. I've talked to a lot of players around the league and they said once the game started, it was just another game. But I never felt it was. I enjoyed every minute of it."

(Kozerski, 42, is the head football coach at Holy Cross High School in Covington, Kentucky. He teaches algebra, geometry, trigonometry and pre-calculus, and is certified to teach physics. During his playing days, he hunted, fished, and worked with tools. But that's all changed. "What do you mean what hobbies do I have? I'm coaching football, taking inventory of equipment, and watching guys lift weights.")

Chance Brockway

Poetry in Motion

¶Eddie Brown, wide receiver (1985-'91)

How many times did quarterback Boomer Esiason drop back and unleash a bomb to No. 81 streaking down the sideline? Plenty. The highly-explosive receiver spent seven years tormenting defensive backs with his silky-smooth, steady-Eddie style. Brown's career yards (6,134) and catches (363) rank fourth and fifth in club history, and his 1,273 receiving yards in 1988 stood as the team record until Chad Johnson (1,355) shattered it in 2003. But Brown needed only 53 catches to accomplish the feat—his season average of 24.0 yards per reception in '88 remains a franchise record—while Johnson's mark came courtesy of 90 catches.

College: University of Miami
Hometown: Miami, Florida
Height: 6-0,
Weight: 185
Pro Bowls: 1

With his burst off the line of scrimmage, quick acceleration downfield, leaping, acrobatic catches, open-field elusiveness, and pillow-soft hands, Brown was poetry in motion. An All-State quarterback/defensive back in high school, he worked with Play-Doh to strengthen his hands, becoming the consensus NFL Rookie of the Year in 1985 with 53 catches for 942 yards (a 17.8-yard average).

"The offense is an explosive offense," Brown said at the height of his career. "They tend to put me in motion a lot, so I am able to move around and make adjustments on my routes."

Because Brown was a threat to go all the way every time he touched the ball, head coach Sam Wyche devised all sorts of ways to free him up. He'd take pitches and run flanker reverses. He'd run crossing routes over the middle. But his specialty was the streak, the fly patterns and "go" routes where he'd dust defenders with his blazing speed.

There were days when Brown, a No. 1 draft pick (13th overall) in 1985, resembled a true Miami Hurricane.

Brown (left) in a celebratory pose from 1989 and (right) eluding Steelers Dwayne Woodruff and Donnie Shell after an Esiason pass.

194

He's as good a blocker at his position as you can find in the NFL. He's always looking for a chance to cut somebody.

—Mike Stock, Bengals receivers coach

Bill Garlow

Like on November 6, 1988, when he caught seven passes for a club-record 216 yards in a 42-7 home victory over the Pittsburgh Steelers.

That was a special game, but his most memorable moment came on a 69-yard TD catch in a 20-17 overtime victory over Washington in the 1988 regular-season finale that clinched home-field advantage throughout the playoffs for the Super Bowl-bound Bengals.

And let's not forget that funniest-home-videos moment during a 10-catch, 178-yard, 2-TD performance in a 21-16 victory over San Diego in September of 1990, when he was the AFC Offensive Player of the Week.

"It was a ball that was thrown to me and I thought I had it when my hands came down," Brown said. "But the ball hit me on the top of my head. As I turned around with my arms out, the ball just dropped right into my hands. I wasn't even looking."

A television commercial for the United Parcel Service asks: "What can Brown do for you?" Teammates, coaches, and fans knew the answer. Eddie Brown could dominate a game.

(Brown, 41, works for Ferraro & Associates, a law firm in Coral Gables, Florida. His hobbies are fishing, basketball, drawing, and golf.)

> **It didn't seem like he was moving that fast, but he was.**
>
> **—Eddie Edwards**

Bill Waugh

Diamond in the Rough

¶Joe Walter, offensive tackle (1985-'97)

Joe Walter has Paul Bunyan's mammoth size and Mother Teresa's heart of gold. But something deep inside motivated him on the football field more than the presence of teammate Anthony Munoz and offensive line coach Jim McNally ever could—that relentless beast known as fear. "I was always afraid of failure," Walter said. "That was the biggest key to me. Being drafted in the seventh round, kind of being a diamond in the rough so to speak, there were a lot of things driving me to be successful."

College: Texas Tech
Hometown: Garland, Texas
Height: 6-7,
Weight: 298

Ol' Joe navigated the rough water of the NFL like Huckleberry Finn rode his raft. He showed guts and grit by overcoming major operations to both knees, providing the Bengals with 13 seasons of excellence at right tackle, tying Hall of Famer Munoz for most seasons played by a Cincinnati offensive linemen.

Driving him all those years was the prospect of getting cut. To overcome his fear, he transformed himself into the Fuller Brush Man every summer. "I considered myself, honestly, a salesman," Walter said. "I went into every training camp thinking, I've got to sell myself to the club to make it here."

The 181st pick of the 1985 draft, Walter established himself as a force with his quick feet, long arms, and great strength. He was so impressive his rookie camp that the club cut sixth-round choice Eric Stokes. After

backing up Mike Wilson and Bruce Reimers for a season, Walter rotated with Brian Blados and finally seized the starting job midway through the 1986 season. He prospered by having the game's top player and teacher to lean on—the M&M duo of Munoz and McNally.

"I owe everything to those two guys," Walter said. "I watched, listened, and learned from them. Anthony is the best-ever offensive tackle. No comparison. He had unbelievable athleticism for his size. There's nothing you can say bad about the guy. Everything is just superior. Anthony and Jim McNally taught me the technique and the work ethic it took to be good. I loved the

At right, the gargantuan Walters scans the enemy front, sealing off attackers from his quarterback. "I loved the game," he said, "and took pride in what I did..."

Despite a 35-23 loss at Dallas in1991, the game was special for Walter. "There's Randy White in his frog stance across from me, and there's 'Too Tall' with the longest arms in America. Those were my idols. I was just in awe."

Chance Brockway

199

game, took pride in what I did and didn't want to fail."

There was no failure in a 28-24 victory at Philadelphia on September 11, 1988. The Eagles had that great defensive line of Reggie White, Jerome Brown, Mike Pitts, and Clyde Simmons. White ranks second on the NFL's career sacks list with 198, but Walter shut him out that day.

"That game sticks out because we kept everybody at bay," he said. "I was *mano y mano* with Reggie and he didn't get a sniff. Reggie swung his big right arm like a club. I just tried to stay away from that, keep him away and not let him get in close to my body to be able to move me out of there."

As fate would have it, Walter missed out on playing in the Super Bowl. He started every regular-season game, but suffered a torn left ACL in the finale against Washington. Defensive end Charles Mann used an "up-and-in" move on him. "When I spun, my foot stayed caught in the turf, and then pop goes the weasel," Walter said.

As the final seconds ticked off the clock and his teammates began celebrating the 20-17 overtime victory that secured home field advantage throughout the playoffs, Walter stood on crutches just beyond the end zone near the tunnel outside the locker room at Riverfront Stadium with his knee encased in ice.

"You work so hard and I had such a great year that you feel cheated that you couldn't play in the Super Bowl," he said. "Walking around Miami on crutches was not a fun thing."

Quarterback Boomer Esiason remembers feeling awfully glad about a 21-14 victory over Cleveland in 1990 that clinched the AFC Central Division title. The Bengals blew a 14-0 halftime lead, but rallied on Eric Ball's 48-yard TD reception in the fourth quarter.

"We were concerned," Esiason said, "so much so that I found myself avoiding our right tackle on the sidelines. Joe is an emotional player and in the second half he wanted to rip someone's head off. I didn't want it to be mine."

Esiason, angry at how the Bengals released Walter in October 1997 by phone, wore Walter's No. 63 on the back of his helmet. "It could have been handled with more dignity," Esiason said. "That's no way to treat a guy who has been so diligent. And it's not like we need more guys like that, huh? Joe Walter was what's right in this dressing room."

(Walter, 41, is assistant vice president of Boone National Bank in Burlington, Kentucky. He's a loan officer specializing in business development and community involvement. His hobbies are family and golf.)

Chance Brockway

The Rock

¶David Fulcher, strong safety (1986-'92)

He was big and he was bad. How big and how bad? Very. At 6 feet, 3 inches and 238 pounds, David Fulcher is believed to be the largest strong safety in NFL history. And he got his nickname—"Fo-Rock"—at Arizona State when he obliterated a wide receiver from New Mexico State. "The guy laid there for a while, then got up and was dizzy," Fulcher said. "Then he said, 'Man, I feel like I ran into a rock.' My teammates just started calling me 'Rock.' A lot of people, when they pronounce my last name, say 'Fo-cher,' so I just put the 'Fo' in front of 'Rock.' "

College: Arizona State
Hometown: Los Angeles, California
Height: 6-3, Weight: 238
Pro Bowl: 3

In a Bengals' career that spanned seven seasons, Fulcher was Dr. Jekyll and Mr. Hyde on the field. Half man. Half monster. Off the field, he's a prince in gym shoes. His 31 interceptions ranks third in team history behind Ken Riley (65) and Louis Breeden (33), but it was his ability to hit and punish people that earned him respect among teammates and struck fear in the hearts of opponents. Fulcher would salivate at the thought of wide receivers coming over the middle. "I tried to be intimidating. I tried to make the people I bumped up against know that David was going to be a force on the football field," Fulcher said. "I loved playing against Haywood Jeffires (Houston Oilers) and Webster Slaughter (Cleveland Browns). They made me feel good when they came across the middle. They played at a very high level, but had some very big mouths. They were always trying to stir things up. When they start talking too much, David wanted to put their mouths to rest."

Fulcher, a third-round draft choice in 1986, would never have been a Bengal had it not been for Ricky Hunley. Hunley, an All-America linebacker from the University of Arizona, was the club's top pick in '84. When contract negotiations remained stalled into September, Hunley's rights were traded to Denver.

Fulcher was the defensive heart of the late 1980s when the Bengals won two divisional titles in three years—his Pro Bowl years.

202

Charlie Steinbrunner

Play me, don't weigh me.

—David Fulcher

Skip Peterson

205

Fulcher calls himself "the Bengals' experiment" because he declared for the draft after his junior season at Arizona State. At the time, the Bengals weren't used to dealing with players coming out early.

"I was born and raised in L.A., and it would have been great to play for my hometown team. But I was drafted by the Bengals and I was happy about it. They needed a strong safety at the time. They put me in there and told me, 'It's yours to lose.' With that attitude, I knew I was going to be there for quite a while."

Fulcher gave three reasons why the Bengals' 20-17 overtime victory over the visiting Washington Redskins in the 1988 regular-season finale was his most memorable game. It cemented his first berth in the Pro Bowl, earned the Bengals home field advantage in the playoffs, and served as a springboard to Super Bowl XXIII.

"It was a game that changed my life," Fulcher said. "It was my third year in the league, but I wasn't recognized throughout the league. And then in my third year, I was mentioned among the elite safeties, guys like Ronnie Lott, Dennis Smith, and Kenny Easley. All of a sudden, here David is right in the thick of 'em. Everything came down to one game, and sure enough, it happened."

His most memorable moment?

"It was the time they called my name during the introductions at the Super Bowl," he said. "Walking out of the tunnel at Joe Robbie Stadium, making sure I did not trip on the turf and fall down."

Fulcher possessed a running back's speed and a linebacker's appetite for hitting...like a rock. But for every wicked lick he dished out on the field, he showed off his soft heart away from the action.

"Football is a violent game," he said. "But once the game is over, you leave your fearsome self on the field and the teddy bear comes out. Off the football field, I was always a person that served in the community. The Bengals could always count on David to be there in a time of need for the people in Cincinnati.

"When fans hear my name, I want them to remember that when that guy stepped out on the field, he was committed to playing the game, loved playing the game no matter how much money was being made, and gave it his all. I laid it on the line and didn't hold anything back."

(Fulcher, 40, is a marketing executive for Summit Financial Group in the Cincinnati suburb of Kenwood. He added to his collection of remote control cars when his wife got him an H2 Hummer for Christmas 2003. His other hobbies are golf, basketball, softball and fishing.)

> I tried to intimidate. I tried to make the people I bumped up against know that David was going to be a force on the field.
>
> —David Fulcher

Bill Garlow

207

Fast Company

¶Eric Thomas, cornerback (1987-'92)

Eric Thomas hung tough against wide receiver Jerry Rice, the San Francisco 49ers great, until the bitter end. That's when the dream turned into a nightmare for the rookie cornerback. It was September 20 in strike-torn 1987, and the Bengals were thoroughly outplaying San Francisco at Riverfront Stadium.

College: Tulane
Hometown: Sacramento, California
Height: 5-11,
Weight: 185
Pro Bowl: 1

They had the 49ers by the throat, poised for the kill, but forgot to squeeze. Unable to run out the clock with a six-point lead on a possession that began at Cincinnati's 45-yard line and 54 seconds remaining, the Bengals gave up the ball at their 25-yard line with :02 on the clock—just enough time for 49ers quarterback Joe Montana and the incomparable Rice to work their magic. A trio of 49ers receivers lined up to the left. On the right, Thomas found himself matched one-on-one with Rice. It's called getting schooled. Rice caught the game-tying TD, and Ray Wersching's extra point completed the 27-26 shocker that nearly got Bengals head coach Sam Wyche fired on the spot.

"I wasn't just going against Jerry Rice," Thomas said. "I was going against (49ers coach) Bill Walsh, one of the greatest offensive minds in football. He knew who I was, and he knew the experience that I had, and it wasn't a lot. So he said, 'Hey, let's see if we can find a way to get Jerry matched up against the rookie.' That's just great coaching.

"Here I am, a young rookie and almost feeling like I had lost the game. But at the same time, I *didn't* lose the game. I actually played pretty well. Jerry caught a couple passes, but I broke up a couple on him. I had a chance early on in my career to learn what competitive greatness was about. Jerry Rice epitomized that term."

Thomas had three tackles and swatted away five passes that day, growing from the Rice episode to

Thomas had been a sprinter in college but once in Cincinnati he soon learned that technique counted as much as speed.

I welcomed being picked on because I wanted to make plays.

—Eric Thomas

became a Pro Bowler the following year when he grabbed seven interceptions as the Bengals barged into the Super Bowl.

"Cornerback is a technique position," Thomas said. "You can't have all the speed and size and think that's all it's going to take. You have to be able to change directions. Your hips have to be ultra smooth. Once I learned how to play the position, I took advantage of what I brought to the table, which was great speed.

"When I came into the league, people had doubts about me and I struggled a little my rookie year. But cornerback, next to quarterback and left tackle, is the hardest position in the league to be successful at early on. After I got on the field and learned what I could do and couldn't do, I thought I developed well.

"Your success always depends on your ability to react," Thomas said. "You don't run to routes. You *react* to routes. That's the challenge. I welcomed being picked on because I wanted to make plays."

A second-round draft pick out of Tulane, where he was a sprinter and long-jumper on the track team, Thomas learned to harness his speed under Bengals defensive coordinator Dick LeBeau.

"Everything you do as a sprinter is based on building a powerful, straightaway long stride," LeBeau said.

"A defensive back needs quick, short strides. He needs to keep his speed under control until he reads the keys that determine where he's supposed to go. *Then* comes the burst of speed."

"I was blessed," Thomas said. "I had a guy who played the same position I played. He taught me the nuances that I wouldn't have gotten from somebody else. The stance, the releases, I learned from Dick."

The turning point in Thomas' career came in the spring of 1990 when he blew out his right knee playing basketball. It usually takes a year to recover from reconstructive surgery, but Thomas' return in December inspired the team on its drive to the AFC Central Division title.

Let the record show that E.T. never phoned home, crying for help.

"I tell guys now, 'Never let yourself get out of shape. You do everything you can to keep your body in tip-top shape so you can play 10 years, and when all is said and done, you can say it was a great experience.'"

(Thomas, 40, is a personal trainer at Club Champions in the Cincinnati suburb of Loveland, and he can be heard weekdays from 5-7 p.m. on WDBZ-AM (1230) "The Buzz" in Cincinnati. "I still lift weights and work out," he said. "I take pretty good care of myself. I don't look at it as a hobby. It's a lifestyle.")

A Different Duck

¶Lee Johnson, punter (1988-'98)

College:
Brigham
Young
Hometown:
Dallas, Texas
Height: 6-2,
Weight: 200

December 7, 1998, is a day that will live in infamy for Lee Johnson. Oh, there were others, but this was Armageddon. The effervescent and funky punter, who attacks life with cup-runneth-over enthusiasm, who always speaks his mind, who never met a person he didn't like—except for New England head coach Bill Belichick—got axed after 11 seasons in Cincinnati. Following a 33-20 home loss to the Buffalo Bills, Johnson questioned management and said if he had Bengals season tickets, he'd probably sell them.

The next day, with Paul Daugherty's column splashed in *The Cincinnati Enquirer*, Bengals president Mike Brown fired Johnson, marking the breakup of "The Three Amigos" (kicker Doug Pelfrey, long snapper Greg Truitt, and Johnson).

"We were tight," Johnson said about the trio that was inseparable for five seasons. "But I blew that. We were getting our face crushed and the whole city was blowing up on Mike, and I said some stupid things after the Buffalo loss, and it just ruined the whole thing.

"I was just saying some things I thought were pretty simple. No anger at all. Then I read 'em in the paper the next day, and I'm like, 'Oh, my gosh.' If I said that, and I'm sure I did, I'll take it. I said it. The way he wrote it was, 'Wow, I blew this one.' It was a mess. I called Mike the year after and we patched it up. I told him I was sorry, nothing against him. I'm convinced if I hadn't said that, I could still be a Bengal."

Instead, he became a Patriot, a Minnesota Viking, and a Philadelphia Eagle, grudgingly shutting down his 18-year career following the 2002 season as the third most prolific punter in NFL history behind Sean Landeta and Jeff Feagles with 1,226 attempts for 51,979 yards, good for a 42.4-yard average.

Johnson, who holds the Super Bowl record for longest punt (63 yards against San Francisco in Super Bowl XXIII) punted in 259 regular-season games, but just nine playoff games.

Johnson's tenure was so long in the NFL that when he signed with the Pats in 1999, the players called him 'Coach.' When they found out he was a player, they changed it to 'Gramps.'

I never was a kicker with great technique. I was always a power guy. Just give me the ball and let me beat the crap out of it. That was always my motto.

—Lee Johnson

Chance Brockway

213

Translation: He played on some very bad teams. Former *Cincinnati Post* beat reporter John Donovan called him the "Charlie Brown of the NFL, a likeable loser who has had the misfortune of playing for teams with double-digit losses and dogs at skill positions."

It didn't start out that way for Johnson. Picked in the fifth round (138th overall) by Houston, he punted barefoot for the Oilers for nearly three seasons, then it was on to Cleveland for the last three games of 1987 and the first three games of 1988. Waived by the Browns on September 21 that year, a Wednesday, Johnson was claimed by the Bengals that Friday, but didn't know it.

The Bengals, unhappy with Scott Fulhage, wanted Johnson to punt that Sunday against the hated Browns. But nobody could find him. "Crazy story," said Johnson, recalling the origin of his only Super Bowl season. "I was traveling home to Utah from Cleveland when the Bengals claimed me off the waiver wire, and I was totally unaware of it. The highway patrol was trying to find me all the way home through Nebraska and Wyoming, which was weird because I was in a red Chevy Blazer. I get home on a Sunday, turn on the TV, the Bengals are playing the Browns, and they're saying that they're looking for me. That's how I found out I was claimed by the Bengals."

Johnson battled the cold-weather elements by wearing a shoe. It helped him gain consistency, but never to the point where he was satisfied. He was motivated by a fear of failure. The self-inflicted pressure he faced in the high-anxiety world of punting constantly stressed him out and nearly overwhelmed him.

"I like competition. And I'm never

had an agent, so he negotiated his own contracts. He crossed the picket line during the 1987 players strike. And between practices during his tenure in Cincinnati, he'd make telephone calls to his broker. No wonder former Bengals head coach Bruce Coslet called him "a different duck."

His boundless enthusiasm for everything came with a price, however, because "that's what got me cut in New England" after five games into 2001. "Bill Belichick thought football wasn't important enough to me. I'm still bitter about that. I felt bad being a jerk. When somebody comes up to talk to me, I've got to say: 'Hey, how ya doing?' Belichick thought I just didn't care. Eighteen years and not care? My life was consumed by football. My wife hated me during the season.

"I was just always looking for the perfect punt, the perfect game. Thank goodness I got into stocks because football would have killed me. Now I could spend time in between practice doing my stocks. It'd take me away. If it didn't, I'd go crazy."

(Johnson, 42, is a self-employed stock trader in Alpine, Utah, where he lives with wife Shelly and their six children. Hobbies? "I'm either with my kiddies on a road bike or mountain bike, hiking or skiing. Anything to make me a better athlete.")

happy with my performance," he said. "But I'm not a natural in that I really don't want the frickin' ball with two seconds left on the free-throw line. So I found every punt very nerve wracking. But yet I kept wanting to play."

The three passions in Johnson life are football, family, and finances—not necessarily in that order. He never

Chance Brockway

The Ickey Shuffle

Ickey Woods, running back (1988-'91)

College:
Nevada-Las
Vegas
Hometown:
Fresno,
California
Height: 6-2,
Weight: 232
Pro Bowls: 1

The Bengals have lost 145 of 208 games since their last playoff season in 1990. That's the bad news. The good news: Fans still cling to two fond memories—the autumn of 1988 and the Ickey Shuffle. The Super Bowl season and the touchdown dance will never be forgotten. There was electricity in The Jungle at Riverfront Stadium and there was magic on the AstroTurf as rookie Ickey Woods rushed for 1,066 yards, 15 touchdowns, and a league-high 5.3-yard average, shuffling into the hearts of teammates, coaches, fans and the front office, nesting forever in Bengals lore.

"What I want fans to think and what they're going to think are two different things," said Woods, whose career was tragically derailed by three knee operations. "I want them to think I was a great ball player who brought a lot of fun to the game. But what they'll think about is the Shuffle."

It began on September 25, 1988, in a 24-17 home victory over Cleveland as the Bengals ran their record to 4-0. Woods had flown his mother in from California and showed her the dance he had been practicing. It was unique, just like him.

"It's just something I made up," he said. "My mom and I were sitting around, then I was up messing around and told her I was going to do it. That's how it all started. I didn't really get a reaction from fans the first time because nobody knew what I was doing. As I was able to score more times that year, we wanted to put a name to it. It started off as the Ickey Shake. Then the media gave it the name, the Ickey Shuffle, and it kind of stuck."

After scoring, Woods faced the end-zone, hopped from one foot to the other, and then, on his last hop, spiked the ball. The Shuffle later moved to the sideline so the Bengals could avoid penalties under the league's "no demonstration" rule.

216

My style? Punish 'em in the first half, go around 'em in the second half.

—Ickey Woods

Bill Garlow

217

Free safety Solomon Wilcots, a Los Angeles-based broadcaster for CBS Sports, laughed with skepticism when Woods auditioned the Shuffle for teammates in the locker room before the Cleveland game.

"Ickey said, 'This is what I'm going to do in the end zone.' I said, 'Dude, there is no *way*. You'll be embarrassed. You've got to come up with something better.' He did it in the locker room, then did it in the game. It became such a craze that a few weeks later Paul Brown started doing it in the locker room.

"I was like, 'Oh, my God, you've got the old man doing the dance. It's official.' That's the charisma Ickey Woods has. He's got that effervescent quality about him that other people are drawn to. He wasn't trying to show up the opponent. He was just trying to have fun. It made that year, which is, in my mind, still very special."

Born Elbert Woods on February 28, 1966, his brother called him "Eee-Eee," which reminded their mother of a cartoon character. Thus, the nickname "Ickey." After leading the nation in rushing with 1,658 yards as a senior at UNLV in 1997, Woods was picked in the second round of the '98 draft (31st overall).

Here was a laid-back Californian, who played in Las Vegas and sported a long ponytail, coming to a sleepy, conservative river town. Doubters,

Bill Waugh

219

critics, and skeptics uttered the same he-won't-last-long refrain.

Well, The Ickster is still living here after all these years. Lucky for him, he had a pair of defensive backs—Wilcots and Eric Thomas, California natives themselves—who took him under their wing. "Solomon and I knew that coming to Cincinnati, people were going to be shocked," Thomas said. "They weren't ready for this jock with long hair hanging down his back. There was going to be an adjustment period, so we sort of anchored him down, and he was really welcome to it.

"Ickey's one of these guys who can adapt to any situation. You put Ickey in the jungle, the next thing you know he's over there leading the bears and the lions. He's that kind of guy. After Ickey was here two years, he could tell me about places that I'd never

heard of in Cincinnati."

"When Ickey came," said Wilcots, "we said, 'If we can just get this guy to work hard, and get him to live up to his deal, we'll win. We had James Brooks, but it was nice to have a big back. The first thing that impressed Eric and me was how fast he was. We called him 'Twinkle Toes' because he had sweet feet for a big back, and he was both quick and fast. All three of us just hit it off so well. I'm still, to this day, drawn to Ickey because of his charisma."

After a brilliant rookie season, highlighted by a 102-yard, two-TD rushing performance in a 21-10

Above photos are from the AFC title game win over Buffalo in January of 1989. Above left, Ickey's 4th quarter TD, and at right, he celebrates after the game with teammate Stanford Jennings.

220

victory over Buffalo for the AFC title, Woods looked to keep the momentum going in '89. But September 17 was the day the music died.

In a 41-10 triumph over visiting Pittsburgh, on a play called "18 Boss," Woods took a handoff from Boomer Esiason, blasted off right tackle, and found an open lane to the outside. Steelers free safety Thomas Everett hit Woods, knocking him to the concrete carpet, and blowing up his left knee.

He played only 19 more games, gained just 365 more rushing yards and scored just 10 more TDs, and he was finished after the 1991 season with career numbers of 332 carries for 1,525 rushing yards (4.6) and 27 TDs in just 37 games.

No sooner had he said hello to the NFL than he was forced to say goodbye. Oh, my, how the franchise suffered. From the 12-4 Super Bowl season to 8-8, 9-7, and, finally, 3-13. We, the people of Cincinnati, never got to Shuffle enough.

"The first couple of years I was out of the game, it was tough," Woods said. "But I didn't feel cheated. You can't harp on the past. You've got to move on."

(Woods, 38, was named head coach of the Cincinnati Sizzle women's football team in November of 2003. His wife, Chandra, is a member of the squad. The Sizzle begins play in the spring of 2005 as an expansion team in the National Women's Football Association, which bills itself as the largest full-contact football league in the world for women. Woods is also a personal trainer at Schwartz Laboratories in Cincinnati, and other fitness facilities in the area.)

Nuts and Bolts

¶Harold Green, halfback (1990-'95)

Harold Green wasn't flamboyant or even flashy. He was a quiet, serious guy who showed a nice blend of speed and power on the field with a style that was, well, nuts and bolts, which was what Green called it. "I was always considered an all-purpose back. I prided myself on my work ethic and being a player who could make a difference on a dismal team, a guy who tried to get the organization on track."

College: South Carolina
Hometown: Columbia, South Carolina
Height: 6-2, Weight: 222
Pro Bowls: 1

Green experienced both peaks and valleys during a turbulent, six-year career in Cincinnati. He led the Bengals in rushing for four seasons and reached the Pro Bowl after a 1,170-yard season in 1992. He tasted the playoffs as a rookie, then endured five straight losing seasons in which the team compiled a 21-59 record.

A second-round draft pick in 1990, Green arrived with a scowl after holding out in a contract dispute as a rookie. "I was young then," he said. "I didn't understand how a team could draft you in the second round and be so slow in the negotiating process. It was immaturity on my part, not realizing the business nature of the game."

Green felt like a kid on Christmas morning that first season when the Bengals went 9-7, won the AFC Central Division, then beat Houston before losing to the Raiders in the AFC Divisional Playoffs.

"I thought things were going to be that way for a long time," Green said. "When you have players like Anthony Munoz, Boomer Esiason, James Brooks, Eddie Brown, Tim McGee, and Rodney Holman as the nucleus of the team, you're like, 'Man, we're going to be *good*. We're not going to falter. I'm going to have an opportunity as a young player to be on a playoff-contending team year in and year out.' But that was not the case."

Green didn't know the club was on the verge of a massive transition. Brooks and fullback Ickey Woods were gone after the '91 season and head coach Sam Wyche was fired.

"I prided myself on a good work ethic," Green said. "I'd get together with Sterling and Shannon Sharpe, two South Carolina guys, in the offseason, and we worked hard at the intangibles—the commitment of taking care of your body."

222

❝Harold had exceptional feet. He could make you miss. The more opportunities you gave him, the more he made of those opportunities.

—Jim Anderson, running backs coach

223

To make matters worse, Munoz retired after the '92 season; Esiason was traded to the New York Jets, also after '92, to make room for David Klingler; and Dave Shula struggled with the responsibility of being the youngest head coach in the league. Green's friendship with Esiason grew, but the relationship was difficult at first.

"My rookie year, Boomer was like, 'Man, look at this guy. He doesn't say anything. He just goes out and bashes guys' heads,' " Green said. "It was a compliment, but I thought he was trying too hard to find out what made me tick. Then we got to know each other well and grew on each other. He'd say, 'OK, rookie, we need something from you. Get this first down.' That's how he was."

Green entered '92 with more enthusiasm and determination than ever. He wanted to showcase his talent, and did, with five 100-yard rushing games culminating in a 190-yard effort against visiting New England on December 20.

"It was very cold that day," Green said. "But everything just clicked. We were a dismal team, up and down and sporadic. A lot of us were looking into each other's eyes, not being able to get a clear-cut answer of who's going to be around."

Green stuck for three more years. The club tried to deal him before the '95 season when it drafted Ki-Jana Carter No. 1 overall. "Shula came to me in training camp and said, 'Now "H", I really appreciate what you're doing. I know we haven't hit on all cylinders at times, but I want you to know I respect you as a player. You're still a team leader here. I just would ask you to embrace this young man (Carter) and try to show him everything you know and mentor him because he's young.'

"I accepted that. Before the conversation ended, he said, 'I know you're still looking to go elsewhere. We're looking to make a trade for you to Kansas City or L.A.' Camp was winding down and that's when Ki-Jana got hurt."

Green, whose offseason workout partners were Sterling and Shannon Sharpe, became a fine receiver out of the backfield. The skill prolonged his career. He spent 1996 with the St. Louis Rams and 1997-'98 with Atlanta, helping the '98 Falcons reach Super Bowl XXXIII, where they lost to Denver, 34-19, prompting his retirement.

(Green, 36, is senior vice president of operations for Pro Bowl Motors, an upscale auto dealership in Columbia, South Carolina. He also works part time in career development for the University of South Carolina. His hobbies are "family, fishing, bowling, and golf.")

Dr. Jekyll and Mr. Hyde

¶Carl Pickens, wide receiver (1992-'99)

College:
Tennessee
Hometown:
Murphy,
North
Carolina
Height: 6-2,
Weight:206
Pro Bowls: 2

To celebrate the $8 million the Bengals handed him in combined signing bonus and salary on September 11, 1999, Carl Pickens neither danced on Fountain Square nor popped open the Dom Perignon. Pickens did something only he would do. He fired his agent for insubordination. With two contracts totalling $35 million, Steve Zucker made Pickens rich beyond his wildest dreams but committed the unpardonable sin of being unable to free Pickens from his perceived penitentiary in Cincinnati.

Oh, Pickens re-hired Zucker after another agent, Hadley Engelhard, got him a contract in Tennessee in 2000. But dropping the ax on Zucker spoke volumes about Pickens. For all his accomplishments as a Bengals' wide receiver—he holds career records for receptions (530) and touchdown catches (63), and ranks second in career receiving yardage (6,887)—his attitude rubbed the glitter right off the record book.

"He was never happy in Cincinnati —never," Zucker said. "I tried to make it where he could be happy, but it was impossible. Mike Brown and I have a very good relationship. The Bengals gave him a lot of money for just one season of a five-year deal. Carl said, 'You made me stay here.' I said, 'You're leaving a lot of money in Cincinnati.' He said, 'I don't want to play here anymore....' "

Athletically, Pickens was incredibly gifted. Part swan. Part shark. He was a world class high jumper who played both ways—wide receiver and safety— at Tennessee. And he used his speed, toughness, and dazzling leaping ability to full advantage. His knees would pump. His arms would flail. And he'd climb somewhere north of reality to haul in those Jeff Blake rainbows down the sidelines, over the middle, and on fade patterns in the end zone.

Pickens' best seasons came during his Pro Bowl years of 1995-'96 when he led the club with 99 and 100 catches—the top two seasons in terms of receptions in club history. In '95,

Pickens' quarterback, Jeff Blake, said of him, "He's the kind of guy who can twist his body to be in a position to catch a ball the defensive back's not going to get. You just know he's going to get the ball."

226

The main thing is determination. When the ball's in the air, I want it to be mine.

—Carl Pickens

Bill Reinke

227

he grabbed a single-season team record 17 TD passes, and followed up with 12 in '96, the second most for a season in club annals.

Dave Lapham remembers Pickens' 11-catch, 188-yard, 3-TD performance in a 34-31 victory over Houston at Riverfront Stadium in 1994, when quarterback Jeff Blake threw for 354 yards and four scores. "A high percentage of those catches were high, arcing, Jeff-Blake-jump-ball situations, and Pickens came down with every single one of them," Lapham said. "He could get up so high, and when he got airborne he was so strong he could out-position and out-muscle people. Every ball was *his* ball. That was his mind-set. But he wasn't the greatest team guy."

And that's the knock against him. Pickens never experienced a winning season with the Bengals, who went 40-88 (.313) in his eight years. The losing poisoned him, and his anger and frustration permeated the locker rooms at Spinney Field and Riverfront Stadium.

Did you know that Pickens was the first restricted free agent in history to sign an offer sheet with another club? Yep. Arizona head coach Buddy Ryan tendered him an offer sheet on March 17, 1995—Green Bay also wanted him—but the Bengals matched it and kept him.

"The lack of winning, that's what it was all about," Zucker said. "Carl's a competitor and just wanted to win. That's what drove him. But he didn't think there was the commitment to win (from the organization)...."

Pickens is an accomplished pianist and drummer, but he spurned media, ripped coaches, mystified teammates, and spawned his own contract clause with his Jekyll-Hyde personality. One minute, he'd cut up with TV reporters, take a microphone and conduct funny mock-interviews with teammates. The next minute, he'd intimidate beat writers with insults and laugh as they walked away. Then he'd slump in his locker, speaking in a hushed tone into his cellular phone.

The same guy who showed off his six-figure game checks to security guards was bumming quarters for the soda machine and parking his sports car in the handicapped area at Spinney Field. And when teammates got cut, he'd finger the leftover articles of clothing in their lockers, smelling them and saying cryptically, "You just never know when your time is going to come."

Head coach Bruce Coslet snapped when Pickens was asked if he was a locker room cancer, as former Bengal-turned-broadcaster Solomon Wilcots alleged in 1997. "This guy (Pickens), when he practices, he practices 100 percent," Coslet said. "When he plays, he plays 100 percent...."

Fast forward to December 30, 1999. Pickens called reporters to his cubicle and ripped management's decision to bring back Coslet in 2000. "I'm very shocked." Pickens said. "I mean, he's never had a winning record, and they bring him back for another year. I don't understand that."

Team publicist Jack Brennan issued an apology in Pickens' name. Had Pickens not apologized, he could have been suspended without pay for a game at Jacksonville, costing him $264,706. The incident triggered the formation of an unprecedented "loyalty clause" in Bengals' player contracts.

The collective bargaining agreement with the NFL Players Association allows teams to suspend a player without pay for up to four games for conduct detrimental to the team. But Mike Brown was looking for a way to punish a player without losing him to a suspension. So the Bengals developed the idea of the loyalty clause, which says that a player can lose his signing bonus for making comments that are "derogatory or critical" of the team, its coaches, or its management. In Cincinnati, it's known as the "Carl Pickens clause."

Pickens' reign of terror ended when he was cut on July 20, 2000, but the loyalty clause keeps his memory alive. The NFLPA challenged the clause and lost.

The mere mention of Pickens' name causes former Bengals quarterback Boomer Esiason's blood to boil. "He's everybody's cancer and he shouldn't be in your book," he said. "He created his own island. He was such a negative influence on people."

Exhibit A is defensive tackle Brentson Buckner, who lasted one season with the Bengals (1997), landed in Carolina, and helped the Panthers reach the Super Bowl in Houston. "Buckner told me that when he signed as a free agent with the Bengals, the first person he saw come through the locker room was Carl Pickens, and Pickens said to him, 'Man, if I would have known you were talking to the Bengals, I would have told you not to come here,' " Esiason said. "That just speaks volumes of what Carl was. I thought he was going to be a great player. For a time there, he was very close. But something happened to him, negative-wise...."

(Pickens, 34, lives in Duluth, Georgia, but spends a lot of time with his mom in Murphy, N.C. He draws residual income from a golf course he purchased and sold with partners. He signed a one-year contract with Dallas in 2001 but chose not to report. Pickens plays the piano and drums and does a great impersonation of comedian Richard Pryor, but only for his closest friends.)

No man is an island, but he sure tries.

—Solomon Wilcots on Carl Pickens

Shake 'N' Blake

¶Jeff Blake, quarterback (1994-'99)

It seems like only yesterday we were jammed inside Willie's Sports Cafe in Covington, Kentucky, celebrating the phenomenon known as "Blakemania." Music was blaring, booze was flowing, and "Shake 'n' Blake" T-shirts were selling like hotcakes. The joint was jumpin' with wall-to-wall, shoulder-to-shoulder, elbow-to-elbow craziness for 700 WLW radio's BengalsLine program. All because of a 23-year-old kid who had a gunslinger's swagger, a rifle arm, a ballerina's feet, and a flair for the dramatic. Quarterback Jeff Blake had become an overnight sensation—in defeat.

College: East Carolina
Hometown: Sanford, Florida
Height: 6-0,
Weight: 210
Pro Bowls: 1

Claimed off the scrap heap known as the NFL waiver wire from the New York Jets on August 29, 1994, Blake got his first career start against Dallas on October 30 because David Klingler and Donald Hollas were injured.

Blake nearly engineered an upset of the Cowboys before the Bengals fell, 23-20, at Riverfront Stadium. He fired first-half touchdown passes of 67 and 55 yards to Darnay Scott, who joined Isaac Curtis (1973) as the only Bengals to score on two passes of 50-plus in the same game.

"Literally, it was Blakemania," Bengals announcer Dave Lapham said. "The Monday night show after that game at Willie's was packed, the biggest BengalsLine crowd I've ever seen. It was like the president of the United States was there.

"Here's a guy that came out of nowhere and captured the town's imagination.

Not surprising, Blake still holds the Pro Bowl record for longest pass completion—93 yards and a TD, to Pittsburgh's Yancy Thigpen in 1996.

We ran the course as long as we could. It wasn't long. Two or three years maybe. But it was fun while it lasted.

—Jeff Blake

Chance Brockway

231

I remember talking to (offensive coordinator) Bruce Coslet. I said, 'Obviously, you liked him as a player. You had him with the Jets and now he's here in Cincinnati. You couldn't have known he was capable of this.' Coslet said, 'If I knew, I would have played him sooner.' "

Blake remembers that game vividly. "We were making plays," he said. "That's the key to any game. People were getting open. I had time to throw. We were making plays and having fun."

Say what you want about Blake. That he was cocky and arrogant. That he was too short to see over his linemen. That he worried more about throwing TDs than winning games. That his off-the-field escapades didn't go unnoticed. But never question his confidence, his commitment to being the best quarterback he could be, or his arm strength.

For 10 seasons—six with the Bengals, two with New Orleans, and one each with Baltimore and Arizona—Blake threw the prettiest deep ball in the league. His long passes were rainbows, spirals climbing high into the sky and falling like raindrops down a chimney to Carl Pickens and Darnay Scott.

"I used to describe it as like a

Bill Reinke

232

bomber airplane would open its doors and, *boom*, the ball would come straight down," Lapham said. "Blake gave his receivers a great opportunity to catch the deep ball because of the trajectory. The receivers could see it first and make the adjustment. Defensive backs had a helluva time making a play on his football."

And without the excitement that Blake generated in 1995-'96, when he threw 52 TD passes for teams that finished 7-9 and 8-8, the palace that is Paul Brown Stadium may never have been built, and the Bengals would likely be playing in Baltimore these days.

Blake ranks third in club history in passing yards (15,134), TD passes (93), pass attempts (2,221), and completions (1,240). He holds the Bengals record for completions in a season (326 in 1995) and his 1.5-to-1 ratio of TD passes to interceptions (93 TDs, 62 INTs) is the best in team history. Boomer Esiason ranks second at 1.43-to-1 (187 TDs, 131 INTs) and Ken Anderson is third at 1.23-to-1 (197 TDs to 160 INTs).

But management lost faith in Blake during a turbulent 1997 season. He was benched in favor of Esiason, who retired after spearheading a spectacular 4-1 finish to a 7-9 season. Then the quarterback carousel began—Neil O'Donnell in '98, Blake as the lame duck in '99, then the Akili Smith-Scott Mitchell disaster of 2000.

"They made me the scapegoat for real," said Blake, who bolted to the Saints as a free agent in 2000. "I want fans to remember the high-flying fun, the attack, the deep ball, Blake to Pickens. I don't know why (management) messed that up, but they did. We had a good thing going. We kept it strong for a good three-four years. You're going to have a down year, and the one down year we had, they just dismantled the whole thing. I said after I left, 'I ain't ever coming back.' The only time I stepped foot in Cincinnati was to play. I have not been back to visit one time in five years."

Life had a way of knocking Blake down. But like all good fighters, he always got back up and kept slugging away. He was 5 when his mother, Peggy, 26, died on the shore of a lake at Wekiwa Springs State Park in Florida during a family outing in 1976.

She had saved her sister, Deborah, 17, from drowning. Jeff was playing on a ballfield with his cousins when he heard a commotion and came running. He got there just before she died.

Peggy's mother wanted to adopt Jeff, but Emory, a Canadian Football League player who became a Baptist minister, said no. Father and son forged an unbreakable bond. "It was like a fuse went off within me that

> They had all these little rules like you can't have TV and radio shows because they were afraid of what somebody might say. If you treat somebody good, you don't have to worry what somebody's going to say.
>
> —Jeff Blake

233

I had to prove to them and Jeff and myself that I could deal with the situation," Emory said. "Anything he needed I wanted to give to him. Everywhere I would go, whatever I was doing, I took him with me."

When Blake was in the 10th grade, his godfather, Major League baseball star Tim Raines, bought Jeff a Kawasaki motorcycle. Jeff was taking videotapes to a store when he was sideswiped by a drunk driver. He spent four weeks in traction with a broken arm, broken hip, and 47 stitches in his knee.

In the hospital, Blake dedicated his life to his mother. He would go on to set or tie 32 school records at East Carolina, finish ninth in the 1991 Heisman Trophy balloting, and he became the Jets' sixth-round draft choice in 1992.

"He is a competitor and a winner," said Coslet, the Jets' head coach from 1990-93. "East Caro-

lina was 11-1 his senior season. They came back from huge deficits on the strength of his play. He was fearless and he can throw the heck out of the football. That's a thumbnail sketch of what I can remember. It was the sixth round and, gosh, he was still way up on the board. We said, 'Well, why not? You can't have too many good quarterbacks.'"

Bill Reinke

234

Fastforward to 1994, the year after Coslet was fired by the Jets and hired as the Bengals' offensive coordinator. New York picked Glenn Foley in the seventh round out of Boston College, giving the Jets four quarterbacks— Boomer Esiason, Jack Trudeau, Blake, and Foley.

"I mentioned that the day of the draft my first year back with Cincinnati," Coslet said. "The Jets can't keep four. They were still running the same offensive system in New York the year after I left and I said whoever gets cut is going to be trained in the system and terminology. So I said on draft day, 'Somebody's going to get cut and we need to keep our eyes open.' The Jets waived Blake, we claimed him, and the rest is history."

Blake threw 47 TD passes to Pickens and learned he couldn't overthrow Scott. Blake played brilliantly in a 25-24 victory at Pittsburgh on December 20, 1998, and on the plane ride home, Coslet tried to convince Mike Brown the Bengals could win with Blake. All he needed was a better supporting cast. Brown told Coslet he was going to draft a quarterback.

It turned out to be Smith, with the No. 3 overall pick in the 1999 draft, an incomprehensible error the franchise paid dearly for. "At that point," Bob Trumpy said, "Bruce understood he had no control over which direction this football team was going. That started the end for Bruce. Whoever recommended Akili Smith, and I think a lot of people did, realized what a terrible mistake it was. They coached the hell out of him, as much as they possibly could. And you see the limitations, and Bruce said, 'I can't do this anymore.' "

Coslet resigned on September 25, 2000, after an 0-3 start. Dick LeBeau took over as the head coach and the Bengals signed quarterback Jon Kitna on March 8, 2001, as an unrestricted free agent from Seattle. Smith was released on June 2, 2003, having made $12 million for 215 completions in 461 attempts (46.6 percent) for 2,212 yards, five TDs, and 13 interceptions.

(Blake, 33, was waived by Arizona in February and signed by Philadelphia in May. He lives in Austin, Texas, with his wife, Lewanna, and their children: Emory (12), Torre (10) and Trey (8). They are considering moving back to Orlando, Florida, where they lived during Blake's Bengal years. Blake's father, Emory, is in his 19th year as pastor of Progress Missionary Baptist Church in Sanford. Blake doesn't have much time to pursue his favorite hobby of jet skiing. "There's no relaxing with kids," he said. "I'm a full-time taxi service.")

The Flying Tiger

¶Darnay Scott, wide receiver (1994-'01)

College:
San Diego
State
Hometown:
East
St. Louis
Height: 6-1,
Weight: 204

Every football legend has a defining moment in his career, and Darnay Scott's came on November 9, 1997, when a guardian angel named Boomer Esiason rescued him from the brink of extinction. Scott was a picturesque pass receiver with the kind of smooth, blazing speed that stretched defenses. He showed "alligator arms" at times early in his career on patterns over the middle because he heard footsteps from safeties eager to take his head off. And for every bushel of brilliant catches he made, he'd allow a pass to fall to the floor, frustrating coaches, teammates, fans—and himself.

Former Bengals greats refer to Scott, a second-round draft pick (No. 30 overall) in 1994, as a poor man's Isaac Curtis, because he was a big-play star that twinkled and shined, just not as blinding as the neon Curtis, who could—and did—do it all.

Curtis had that signature over-the-shoulder spike when he scored. But Scott was careful never to draw attention to himself. Head coach Dave Shula once asked Scott why he was never the first player on the field or the last one to leave. "I was born in East St. Louis," he said. "You're never the first one in line or the last one in line. Those are the guys that get shot."

With that upbringing, Scott's whole mindset was to fit in, to not be "the guy." He was content to be the No. 2 receiver, dutifully subservient to the snarling, intimidating Carl Pickens,

and never one to complain about the number of balls thrown his way.

But he always kept teammates guessing as to his whereabouts off the field. Scott—who ranks fourth in Bengals history in catches (386) and fifth in receiving yards (5,975)—is the only receiver in club annals to top the 800-yard plateau in each of his first three seasons, yet management didn't like his brushes with the law, and he had several.

He was arrested in 1996 in San Diego on separate charges of suspicion of possession of a concealed weapon and possession of a loaded firearm in a vehicle. He was arrested again in 1998 in Cincinnati on several

"Amazingly graceful and appallingly erratic," *Enquirer* sports columnist Tim Sullivan once wrote about Scott.

outstanding traffic warrants, and in 2000, he was accused of writing a bad check to a motorcycle shop.

With all that serving as a backdrop, let's go to the RCA Dome in Indianapolis in '97. Scott was benched by a "coach's decision" because he blew off a series of meetings—his only missed start of the season. He dressed, caught one pass for eight yards, and the Bengals rallied for a 28-13 victory spearheaded by Esiason, whose block sprang tailback Corey Dillon for a 46-yard touchdown run.

What happened next saved Scott's career. Scott was going to be an unrestricted free agent at season's end and he needed a dramatic turnaround to get out of the doghouse and into a new contract. A reading from the Book of Boomer: "On my way back from Indianapolis, I called Darnay's agent (Rocky Arceneaux) and said, 'I don't know what you or your client are thinking about, but he's going to ruin a huge payday if he doesn't get his act together. He's probably one step from being booted off this team and you're going to have a hard time finding him a deal next year. You'll get him $800,000, but he deserves a lot more because he's a much better player who is completely off-center right now.' "

Arceneaux spoke with Scott, and Esiason did, too. Esiason took over for Jeff Blake with five games remaining and with the snap of a finger, Esiason and Scott clicked. With Pickens out the remainder of the season with a torn groin muscle, Scott finally got his chance to shine and took advantage of it.

Bill Reinke

Esiason said to Darnay, "Listen, there are professionals and then there are the people who *think* they are professionals. You owe it to your family and yourself to act like one and become one. What is your problem?"

Scott said he was angry about not being taken seriously. "I told him, 'If you have a suggestion, you tell me and we will absolutely figure out a way to get it in the game plan,'" Esiason said. "And then when Pickens —everybody's cancer—went down, I told him: 'I know that Pickens beat into your brain that you're No. 2 and David Dunn was No. 4 and James Hundon was No. 6A. Let me tell you something. You are No. 1 now, my friend.'"

Scott averaged 105.8 yards (22 catches, 423 yards, 3 TDs) the final four games of '97, signed a five-year, $15-million contract in the offseason and sent Esiason a $25,000 check for

Bruce Coslet resigned three games into the season.

Scott cemented his status as a mystery man in August of 2001, with an incident in the parking lot of Rawlings Stadium at Georgetown College when he climbed behind the wheel of an immaculate white Jaguar with Utah license plates.

Utah? Nobody on the club was from Utah. "Darnay, what's the deal with the Utah plates?" a reporter asked.

"Hey, baby," he said, "you've gotta mix 'em and match 'em so that nobody finds you."

With residences in San Diego, St. Louis, and northern Kentucky, Scott made sure the club couldn't find him during the 2002 offseason. So the Bengals terminated his contract on July 9, freeing themselves from the weight of his $3.2 million salary. And that ended the Cincinnati career of this talented player and enigmatic character.

Cystic Fibrosis. Coming off a career-best 1,022-yard season in '99, Scott was supposed to lead a contingent of young stars in 2000. But the season was destroyed on August 1 when Scott suffered a fractured tibia and fibula in his left leg in a freak accident on a play at training camp.

Quarterback Akili Smith struggled with young receivers, didn't get the protection he needed from left tackle Rod Jones, and head coach

(Scott, 32, who grew up with rap superstar Nelly in East St. Louis, played 14 games for the Dallas Cowboys in 2002, catching 22 passes for 218 yards (9.9) and 1 TD. He's living in St. Louis, working out and trying for an NFL comeback. His favorite hobbies are playing video games and basketball.)

Bill Reinke

The Road Grader

¶Willie Anderson, offensive tackle (1996-present)

He's been on the field for more than 8,000 offensive snaps in his pro career, but one play says it all about Willie Anderson. When Baltimore safety Chad Williams intercepted a Jon Kitna pass and raced 98 yards down the right sideline for a touchdown in the Ravens' 27-23 victory in Cincinnati on Dec. 1, 2002, Anderson could have turned into a spectator. Instead, he rumbled across the field from his right tackle position, angling toward the sideline, in an attempt to cut down Williams. Anderson never quite caught up, but he came close. Other teammates had stopped running, but not Big Willie. He didn't quit. That's a fitting epitaph when he decides to call it a career.

College: Auburn
Hometown: Mobile, Alabama
Height: 6-5,
Weight: 340
Pro Bowls: 1

For eight seasons, he's been a symbol of excellence for the franchise, leading the squad in total games (126) and starts (120). His 64 straight starting assignments—the longest active streak on the roster—is a testament to his durability. All his hard work paid off in 2003 when he was voted to his first Pro Bowl, an honor long overdue.

Tailback Corey Dillon had been the club's headliner since 1997, rolling up a franchise-record 8,061 rushing yards, only because "I-71"—Anderson—helped creat daylight. When the honor was announced, Marvin Lewis couldn't wait to tell Anderson, who became only the third offensive lineman in club history to reach the Pro Bowl. Hall of Fame tackle Anthony Munoz made it 11 times and guard Max Montoya three times. So the first-year head coach found the massive tackle in the locker room at Paul Brown Stadium.

"He actually followed me into the bathroom when I was peeing," Anderson said. "I turned around and said, 'What's going on?' He said, 'You made it.' I couldn't stop what I was doing. But when he left, I got on one knee and thanked God."

On bended knee, Anderson promised to send his Pro Bowl bonus money to charity. The minister and congregation at New Jerusalem Baptist Church in Cincinnati had offered a

At the Pro Bowl, Donovan McNabb introduced Anderson and then said, "He should have been here two or three years ago."

240

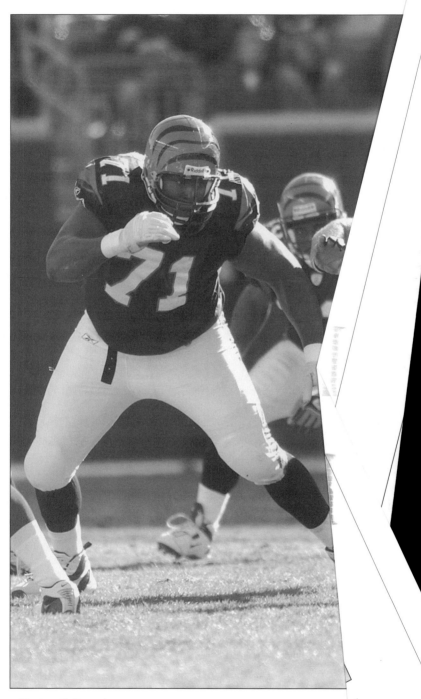

Cincinnati Bengals

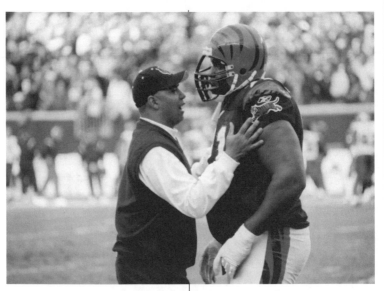

prayer for him the night before, and for that he's eternally grateful. Anderson also said a prayer for his sister, Jackie, who was killed by a drunk driver in Mobile, Alabama, in 1985 at the age of 17 when Willie was 10.

Anderson doesn't tell the story often because it's too painful, but he wanted to let fans know because she played such a critical role in his life. Jackie had begged Willie all day to let her ride his go-kart. Finally, he relented. When he arrived home with friend, a herd of kids came running round the corner to tell him she had st gotten hit.

"We all took off running to see r," Willie said. "I got there and w her body lying in the middle of street. I started stuttering right

about the time I saw her. For years, I had to try to overcome the stigma of being the big stuttering kid. Athletics led me out of that. Jackie helped raise me, and she never got a chance to see me play sports. That's why I look at things and say, 'Hey, there's not a whole lot of stuff people can say or do to affect me in a negative way. There are more important things in life.' "

A three-year starter at Auburn who led the Tigers to a 20-1-1 record in 1994-95, Anderson was a first-round pick (No. 10 overall) as an early-entry junior in the 1996 NFL Draft. Named the NFL's top right tackle in 2002 by The War Room, a scouting service, Anderson sought the league's seal of approval with a Pro Bowl bid. He finally seized it during an 8-8 season under Lewis, whose prophecy came true. When he took over the job from the fired Dick LeBeau in January 2003, Lewis gave this message to Anderson's agent, Terry Bolar, in Georgia: "We're coming in this year to get this team going, and once this team gets going, good things are going to come for Willie."

"I'm just thankful for Marvin Lewis coming here and coaching this team," Anderson said. "I told all the guys: 'If you didn't bring what you brought to the team, people wouldn't have come and watched us.' It's not about me. Everybody wants to say, 'You should have made it (in the past).' I'm thankful it came this way because we were in the playoff hunt. I'll be much more satisfied to be playing in January, though."

On the field, Anderson is a road-grading run blocker and shut-down pass protector, who wears the biggest shoe size (19 EEE) in franchise history. Off the field, he's the club's most active player in civic and charitable endeavors. He was the Bengals' nominee for the NFL Man of the Year award three years in a row (2000-02), donating game tickets in his private suite for underprivileged children, sponsoring dinners for the homeless, and holding Christmas parties at Children's Hospital in Cincinnati.

Because he cares so much for the team and community and because he wanted so badly to reach the playoffs

in 2003, Anderson erupted in anger following the season-ending loss to Cleveland when Dillon threw his equipment into the stands. "Get him out of here, man, because some of that stink is still around here, and you can smell it in close games like the 22-14 loss to the Browns," Anderson said.

"We need passionate guys. If you don't want to be here, get 'em out of here, man. Bye. Good riddance."

Dillon went to New England in a trade, but Anderson is still here, a survivor of the brutal past, seeking a bountiful future. "Hopefully people will see the effort we put forth in 2003 and see that we did exceed a lot of people's expectations," Anderson said.

"Our goal was to make the playoffs, but people outside this organization said we wouldn't win four games. To come in and do what we did in Marvin's first season put us ahead of the curve, so by 2004 we can figure out how to win those three to four ball games that we lost that we should have won."

(Anderson, 29, is in his fourth season of a six-year, $31 million contract. He owns a real estate company, Think B.I.G. Inc. His hobbies include reading, playing basketball and piano, traveling, yacht racing, skydiving, wine tasting, and whitewater rafting.)

This is the new Bengals! A new team! A new era! It starts right now!

— Willie Anderson, screaming inside a sideline huddle, 2003

Demolition Man

¶Corey Dillon, tailback (1997-'03)

It's April 19, 1997, the second round of the NFL Draft is underway and the occupants of the Bengals' War Room, hunkered down at the team's Spinney Field headquarters, are excited because early-entry junior Corey Dillon is still on the board. The Bengals have already taken the pass rusher they want with the 14th pick in the first round—Florida State defensive end Reinard Wilson—but need some insurance for tailback Ki-Jana Carter, who tore his left ACL in 1995. With each selection, the intensity and anticipation grows stronger.

College: Washington
Hometown: Seattle, Washington
Height: 6-1,
Weight: 225
Pro Bowls: 3

As soon as the Atlanta Falcons choose Texas Tech tailback Byron Hanspard 41st overall, the possibility of grabbing Dillon becomes real because everybody knows Arizona is taking quarterback Jake Plummer next. The Bengals' brass suddenly focuses on one man—Dillon, the talented but troubled tailback from the University of Washington coming off a season in which he rushed for 1,555 yards and 22 touchdowns.

Running backs coach Jim Anderson leads the discussion, with input from special teams coach Al Roberts, who had been Dillon's position coach at the University of Washington. He knew this kid the best.

Dillon reminds Roberts of Pro Football Hall of Fame running back Jim Brown, but nobody could have dreamed the 43rd overall draft pick would become the greatest tailback in Bengals history, holding or sharing 18 franchise records, including most rushing yards for a career (8,061), season (1,435 in 2000) and game (278); and most career yards from scrimmage (9,543).

"Dillon was the highest-rated athlete on the board," Roberts said. "He was big, fast, and durable. He was everything we needed out of a big-time running back. It came down to his character, his past, his history." And that picture wasn't pretty.

Seattle newspapers reported Dillon had numerous juvenile arrests, including one for selling crack cocaine to a police officer when he was 15. Dillon was found guilty and

How good was Dillon in his record game against Denver? Ten of his 22 runs were for 2 yards or less, including six runs of zero or minus yards. Other runs were for 34, 31, 21, 37, 30, 14, 65 and 41 yards.

244

> This is a smash-mouth sport and if you're not going full speed, you're going to get hurt. I'm a contact guy. I'm in there to do damage and wear down the defense.
>
> —Corey Dillon

Bill Reinke

245

sentenced to nine months' probation, community service and 10 days in a juvenile detention center. Dillon denied selling drugs. But there is no denying his chiseled physique decorated with profane tattoos. Along with a Grim Reaper on one arm and a "Down and Dirty" message on his chest, there is a naked woman, surrounded by dice, the ace of spades, and the words "Livin' Like A Hustler."

Dillon's shady past makes him a gamble. Bengals president Mike Brown wonders: Would he tear up the league as a rookie like Eddie George? Or would he be just another problem child like Lawrence Phillips? The Bengals don't have long to wrestle with the dilemma.

"We're on the clock now," said Roberts. "It's a 10-minute deal, so we don't have a whole lot of time to hold our butts. Mike looked at me and I said it again, 'Draft him.' And he gave the card to Pete (Brown) and Pete drafted him."

Meanwhile, back in Seattle, Dillon is fuming. He thought, for sure, he was going to the New Orleans Saints with the 10th pick in the first round because Saints coach Mike Ditka had shown the most interest. But Ditka denied Dillon three times, and Dillon arrives in Cincinnati with a chip on his shoulder.

Quarterback Boomer Esiason gets into his head: "It's not how you got

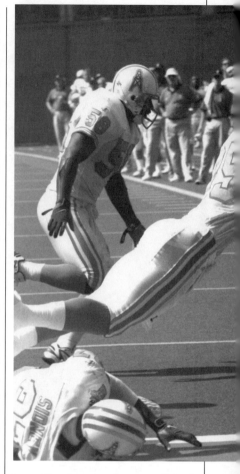

here. It's what you do to stay." And from the beginning, Dillon exerts his strong personality. Head coach Bruce Coslet wants to bring him along slowly behind Carter, but Dillon is in a hurry to become The Man.

"If I don't start, hey, it ain't gonna be like that for long," Dillon said. "I'm not one to sit the bench behind nobody."

246

Dillon doesn't break into the lineup full-time until Week 11 of 1997. He finishes the season with 1,129 rushing yards—third most ever by a Bengal, even though he played only 31 percent of the offensive snaps the first eight games—and is named AFC Rookie of the Year. His 246-yard performance on December 4 against Tennessee smashes the NFL rookie record of 237 set by his boyhood idol, Cleveland's Jim Brown, in 1957.

He earns three Pro Bowl berths, becomes only the fourth player in NFL history to rush for at least 1,000 yards in each of his first six seasons. And he does it with a simple philosophy. "Contact—I love it," Dillon said. "I try to combine my skills—power and speed. And I

Ty Greenlees

247

challenge any defender. That's how I play. Why change? This is the type of sport where you hit or be hit. I'd rather hit you before you hit me."

Asked once to describe his running style, he replied in one word: "Brutal," he said.

Dillon's greatest moment as a pro came against Denver on October 22, 2000, when he set the NFL single-game rushing record of 278 yards in a 31-21 victory over Denver at Paul Brown Stadium, shattering the previous mark of 275 set by Chicago Bears' Hall of Fame legend Walter Payton, against Minnesota in 1977.

Two days later, Dillon's jersey, pants and shoes are taken to the Pro Football Hall of Fame in Canton for display. Dillon gets rewarded with a five-year, $26 million contract on May 11, 2001, apologizing for comments made a year earlier when he said he'd rather "flip burgers" than play for the Bengals.

"God works in mysterious ways," Dillon said. "It's a blessing for me that I didn't get to go in the first round and make the money up front at first

because I wasn't mature enough to handle it. The stage I'm at now, I'm more mature. I'm glad things turned out the way they did. I'm the person I am today because of what happened back in '97. It made me come in here, get focused, work extremely hard, and it paid off. Because I missed it in '97, I made up for it. It's a great accomplishment."

Of course, everyone knows what happens next. Baltimore's Jamal Lewis breaks Dillon's NFL record with 295 yards against Cleveland in 2003, and Dillon's streak of 1,000-yard seasons ends because of a severe groin injury that limits him to 541 yards.

Unable to share the spotlight with emerging star Rudi Johnson, Dillon throws his helmet, shoulder pads and cleats into the stands at Paul Brown Stadium following the 2003 season-ending loss to Cleveland that

left the Bengals at 8-8. He cleans out his locker and, like the Grinch, even takes his nameplate. It's his way of saying goodbye.

The exclamation point comes in March 2004 when he walks onto the set of Fox Sports' Best Damn Sports Show Period, rips the team, reveals his "power struggle" with first-year head coach Marvin Lewis, and cheapshots right offensive tackle Willie Anderson, calling him "a bum."

Dillon finally gets his wish on April 19, leaving a Bengals team with a 34-78 record and 30.4 winning percentage during his seven-year tenure. His trade to New England ends a stellar but stormy career in which he rushes for 8,061 yards and 45 touchdowns, averaging that ugly 4.3 yards per carry and leaving a legacy as a brilliant, belligerent, accomplished, unhappy superstar.

(Dillon, 30, was traded to New England on April 19, 2004, for the Patriots' second-round pick –No. 56 overall–in the 2004 NFL Draft on April 24. The Bengals selected Maryland free safety Madieu Williams. Dillon had two years remaining on a five-year, $26 million contract at the time of the trade. Dillon, wife Desiree and daughter Cameron live in Los Angeles in the offseason.)

Bill Reinke (left) and Ron Alvey

¶Takeo Spikes, linebacker (1998-'02)

Takeo Spikes always had a story that left you smiling. He talked about turning lumps of coal into diamonds, studying quarterbacks' eyes, ripping running backs' heads off, and punishing himself by watching the NFL playoffs on television. But the best Spikes' story was the linebacker-turned-chef tale when he hosted Thanksgiving Day supper for players whose families lived out of town. In 2000, he told beat writers how he planned on fixing all the traditional favorites, plus a bonus dish—barbecued raccoon.

College: Auburn
Hometown: Sandersville, Georgia
Height: 6-2,
Weight:245

A year later, the scribes approached Spikes with a pressing question. Are you going to serve barbecued 'coon for Thanksgiving again this year, Takeo?

"Can't put the 'coon on, man... damn 'coon didn't work out so good last year," he said. Why not? "Can't tell you why, man." In other words, pass the Pepto-Bismol, please.

Perhaps no player in Bengals history had a more fitting name than Spikes. Takeo, pronounced "tuh-KEE-oh," means "great warrior" in Japanese. And Spikes truly was, is, and forever will be a great warrior. He recorded 14.5 sacks, recovered 11 fumbles, forced seven fumbles, intercepted five passes, scored two touchdowns, and became only the third Bengal to earn four team tackling titles, joining defensive tackle Tim Krumrie (five) and linebacker Jim LeClair (four). But

Spikes' feat came in just five seasons, and they were five l-o-n-g seasons in which the Bengals finished 3-13, 4-12, 4-12, 6-10 and 2-14.

The losing tore him up so bad that in March of 2003, after signing a six-year, $32 million offer sheet with the Buffalo Bills, Spikes asked head coach Marvin Lewis not to match it, and Lewis obliged.

"I feel like my time (in Cincinnati) is done," Spikes said. "I did all I can do. I did all that I owed not only to them, but to myself. I just want to win. That's my whole objective. I just want to go somewhere to compete and win."

The Bengals had made Spikes their transition free agent, meaning they

Spikes on hitting the QB: "I want to hit him so that when he gets up, he'll get on his fullback and say, 'Don't let that guy come in here clean.' That's gas in the tank."

250

I dream of that clean shot, coming from the blind side and just killing somebody or going through somebody just to get to the ball carrier. I won't be denied.

—Takeo Spikes

Cincinnati Bengals

251

had the right to retain him by matching any offer sheet he signed with another club, but they wouldn't get compensation if they let him walk. Why didn't the Bengals place the franchise tag on Spikes so they could get compensation in return? Because no club in its right mind would have paid that kind of money—plus first- and third-round draft picks— for Spikes. By divorcing the disgruntled, Lewis sent a message: Either sail with the ship or get your tail overboard.

When you think about it, Spikes was the MVP of the 2003 Bengals.

Had he not shuffled off to Buffalo, then defensive tackle John Thornton, linebacker Kevin Hardy, and cornerback Tory James wouldn't be here. All three were in the Bengals' fold the weekend Spikes bolted—three for the price of one—and they were key ingredients to an 8-8 turnaround season.

Nevertheless, Spikes' former teammates couldn't hide the disappointment of losing their defensive captain. "I'm happy for him because it's what he wants," said linebacker Brian Simmons, a first-round draft pick with Spikes in 1998.

Shannon O'Brien

"But I'm going to miss him. Every side of the ball needs an emotional guy like that."

Spikes was immensely popular from the July day in 1998 when he signed his five-year, $7.53 million contract, then stepped onto the field for his first live drill in which he called the defensive play, sprinted to his left, and intercepted a pass. "What more could a rookie ask for?" he said.

Spikes' karate kicks and darting hand moves after sacks and tackles for loss captured fans' imagination. They won't soon forget his 45-yard fumble return for a TD at Carolina in 2002, or his tackle against Pittsburgh's Jerome "The Bus" Bettis when he grabbed hold of Bettis' shoulder pads and yanked him down with one hand.

But the signature play of Spikes' career came in a 21-10 home victory over Baltimore in 2001. Clinging to a 14-10 lead with the Ravens driving for the go-ahead score, Spikes made a leaping interception of an Elvis Grbac pass intended for tight end Shannon Sharpe and rumbled 66 yards for the first TD of his NFL career.

"A lot of guys on this team look at me," said Spikes. "I needed to step up and make a big play. I got a hand on it and I was off to the races. It was great, man, big time."

Spikes received a game ball, and some 20 players celebrated at a Northern Kentucky nightspot, with the owners sending over a bottle of Dom Perignon—on the house.

Spikes never missed a Bengals game or start due to injury. It took the death of his father, Jimmie Spikes, who succumbed to brain cancer in 2001, to keep Spikes out of the lineup for the only time. The Bengals responded with a 24-14 home victory over Cleveland. "We couldn't let Takeo down," defensive tackle Oliver Gibson said. "He's our guy, our heart."

Said Spikes: "My father lives through me. He came up so hard. The white man told him: 'If you don't go out and plow the field, we'll kick your family out and bring another family in.' He quit school. He worked on Thanksgiving and Christmas. He worked so hard to give all of us the knowledge that 'I'm going to take care of everything. But you have to do us right by going to get your education so you don't have to do what I had to do.' He was blue-collar all the way."

(Spikes, 27, finally reached the Pro Bowl in 2003 as a Buffalo Bill. The final game of his Bengals career came at Buffalo on December 29, 2002—the same day Cinergy Field was imploded. The Bills signed him to a six-year, $32 million contract as an unrestricted free agent. His hobbies include fishing, traveling, and meeting people).

I dream of hitting a running back so hard that his helmet comes off. Then I pick up the helmet and throw it to the head coach.

—Takeo Spikes

253

Mr. Deep Six

¶Chad Johnson, wide receiver (2001-present)

College:
Oregon State
Hometown:
Miami,
Florida
Height: 6-1,
Weight: 192
Pro Bowls: 1

In separate advertising campaigns to promote ticket sales and new uniforms in 2004, the Bengals and Reebok—which holds the exclusive license to manufacture and sell NFL-licensed merchandise—needed star power. The search began and ended with Chad Johnson. Looking up at the billboards featuring Johnson's image, splashed all over Cincinnati, you can tell he's on top of the world as he enters his fourth NFL season. But it wasn't long ago when Johnson was at rock bottom.

He has a simple explanation for how he got to the NFL in the first place, for how he followed his 1,166 receiving yards in 2002 by leading the AFC with a Bengals' record 1,355 yards in 2003, breaking the 14-year-old club record of 1,273 set by Eddie Brown in 1988, and for how he has risen to superstar status.

"I'm not supposed to be here at all," Johnson said. "I might be one out of a million people that would try to do the same thing and use football to get here. I just happened to get through the cracks."

Barely graduating from Miami Beach High School in 1996, he was thrown out of Langston (Oklahoma) University for fighting and not attending class. Then it was off to Santa Monica Junior College, where he played in '97, was academically ineligible in '98, and played again in '99. "It took three years to get out because I couldn't get my grades right," Johnson said. "When it was time to go to a four-year college again, I still was short some credits, so I had to fight to get through school. It's a good thing Oregon State is on quarters. If they weren't, I wouldn't have gotten in there, either."

In his only season of major college football, Johnson caught 37 passes for 806 yards (21.8) and eight touchdowns, including a school-record 97-yard TD against Stanford, and TDs of 4 and 74 yards against Notre Dame in the Fiesta Bowl. His performance caught the pro scouts' attention and Johnson became the Bengals' second-round pick (No. 36

Says Johnson, "Carson should be able to just let it go and let me go get it. I'm not trying to be cocky or talk mess, but I'm going to always be open—always."

> **There are three things that are certain in life. Death, taxes and me trash - talking.**
>
> —Chad Johnson

Cincinnati Bengals

255

overall) in the 2001 NFL Draft. "They called me that one-year wonder at Oregon State," Johnson said. "Once I got to that big stage, that's all I needed."

Johnson's modus operandi, of course, is making guarantees, backing up his boasts with production, and rolling up fines with end-zone celebrations. He guaranteed a victory at Houston in 2002 and the Bengals won, 38-3. Then he guaranteed a victory over the undefeated Kansas City Chiefs in 2003. The psych-job worked with the Bengals prevailing, 24-19, as the Chiefs fell to 9-1.

Johnson drew criticism from Chiefs head coach Dick Vermeil and from some of his Bengals teammates. But the braggadocio garnered headlines from sea to shining sea, focusing attention on Cincinnati, and turned Johnson into a national celebrity and media megastar.

His fine total from the league topped $70,000 in 2003. On the same weekend New Orleans Saints star receiver Joe Horn got hammered with a $30,000 fine for making a choreographed cell-phone call to celebrate a TD against the New York Giants, Johnson held up a sign after scoring against San Francisco that read: "Dear NFL: Please don't fine me again. Merry Christmas."

It cost him a cool 10 grand. Fans love it, but the league doesn't. At the NFL Annual Meeting in Palm Beach, owners came within one vote of unanimous in approving a resolution that automatically penalizes a player 15 yards if he is called for an excessive celebration.

"We think it's time," Bengals president Mike Brown said. "Look at the number of fines this past year

Cincinnati Bengals

(61). It's getting out of hand. We talked to Chad last year about it and he understood that he had to set a better example. Now he'll get his head ripped off by everybody. Players, coaches, the fans. No one wants the penalty."

But everybody wants Johnson, especially the Bengals and Reebok. He's helping sell season tickets, with billboard headlines screaming, "Guaranteed Fun." And he's modeling the club's striking new uniforms that Reebok helped design, with his image splashed along a motto that reads: "The Future Is Here."

We caught a glimpse of what the future holds for Johnson during the Pro Bowl in February. He turned Aloha Stadium into his personal playpen, recording five receptions for 156 yards—second most in the game's history—including a 90-yard TD from Titans quarterback Steve McNair on the AFC's first play from scrimmage. Only the Vikings' Randy Moss (212 yards in 2000) had more receiving yards in a Pro Bowl, and Johnson's catch was the second-longest TD reception in Pro Bowl history behind the 93-yarder from the Bengals' Jeff Blake to the Steelers' Yancey Thigpen in 1996.

"I'm not even playing for the Pro Bowl no more," Johnson said. "The Pro Bowl is a given. I'm playing for the Hall of Fame now. That's my new motto. I want to get inducted while I'm still playing the game."

Johnson became only the second Bengals receiver to catch 90 or more passes in a season—his 90 in 2003 ranked third in club history behind Carl Pickens' 100 (1996) and 99 (1995). And his 10 TD receptions were the most since Pickens had 12 in '96. To shatter Jerry Rice's NFL single-season receiving record of 1,848 yards set in 1995, Johnson must develop a special chemistry with new quarterback Carson Palmer. Johnson said it won't take long.

You can check out their progress when the Bengals host Denver on Monday Night Football on October 25, Cincinnati's first MNF appearance since 1992.

"Everybody on the outside sees what's going on with this organization and the direction we're headed," Johnson said. "It's not even fair about what's getting ready to go on. I wouldn't be surprised if we go to the big dance."

(Johnson, 26, signed a five-year, $25 million contract extension through 2009. He has the No. 1 selling Bengals jersey—No. 85—ranking eighth nationally behind Eagles QB Donovan McNabb. Johnson's favorites: Movie (tie, Chicago and Moulin Rouge); Music and artist (Rap and Trick Daddy); Meal (Baked chicken, yams, macaroni & cheese and green beans.)

"People call me cocky, but that's just me. I'm the 'Mouth of the South.' You know what it does? It puts pressure on myself. With me talking, I can't do anything but back it up.

—Chad Johnson

The Air Apparent

❡Carson Palmer, quarterback (2003-present)

College:
Southern Cal
Hometown:
Laguna Hills,
California
Height: 6-5,
Weight:230

He came out of the womb throwing the football and it's almost like the football gods placed Ken Anderson and Boomer Esiason in a blender, hit the mix button, and the whirring resulted in a concoction called Carson Palmer, the Bengals' quarterback. Palmer has Esiason's big arm, huddle presence and confidence, but isn't much for the glare of the spotlight, and that's Anderson. Palmer welcomes the Midwestern lifestyle over the frenzied pace of Los Angeles, where he had to drive a half hour to go five miles to get a bite to eat. And that, coupled with his enormous talent, makes him a perfect fit to guide the Bengals to a place they haven't been since the 1990 season—the playoffs.

Without hurling his first pass in an NFL regular-season game, Palmer is a Bengals' legend because of the production he's shown leading up to this moment in his storybook career, and the promise he holds for the future as the team's $49 million franchise quarterback. Heck, Carson Palmer limited edition collectible bobbleheads, courtesy of Players, Inc., have already hit stores and are flying off shelves. "You could justify his ranking as a legend," Esiason said, "by the fact that he's at least the guy who's made the most money without playing a down."

Palmer is not David Klingler, the product of a run-and-shoot offense at the University of Houston, and he is not Akili Smith, the immature one-year wonder at the University of Oregon. He is the Golden Boy with the cannon arm, magic touch, laser accuracy, quick feet and picture-perfect release and follow-through

Said Marvin Lewis, "He's very, very talented. He's done nothing since we've drafted him to disappoint any of us. We're excited about him, his future, and his ability to help us offensively."

258

> I'm still young and naive. I expect to win every single game.
>
> —Carson Palmer

Cincinnati Bengals

259

that makes his passes so smooth, so strong, and so effortless that his consistency borders on the robotic.

"I was born to play football," Palmer said. "I love the rush you get out of winning. I'm not going to be jumping around and doing touchdown dances, but I'm definitely going to be high-fiving and, hopefully, be fun to watch."

He was fun to watch at Santa Margarita High School in California, where he threw for 56 touchdowns en route to two state championships (1996-97). He was fun to watch as a four-year starter at the University of Southern California, where a brilliant 2002 senior season—3,942 yards, 33 TDs and 10 INTs—culminated with Palmer capturing the Heisman Trophy.

Palmer's tutor since the seventh grade has been Bob Johnson, head coach of the renown Elite 11 Quarterback Camp and the father of NFL quarterback Rob Johnson. Bob Johnson taught Palmer the nuances of the position, including throwing mechanics and footwork. What a coach can't teach—those delicious intangibles such as desire and leadership—Palmer has.

That's why the Bengals were attracted to him as the No. 1 overall pick of the 2003 NFL Draft. Asked to name the last "sure thing" he saw on a draft board, Bengals head coach Marvin Lewis didn't hesitate: "Carson Palmer and (2003 second-round pick) Eric Steinbach. They both have the ability, physically and mentally, and what's inside of them— that 'want-to' to be great.

"We saw Carson make all the throws we thought he would have to make as an NFL quarterback. They ran quite a few bootleg, waggle-type actions out of their offense at USC and he was accurate with it and moved well. When he had to tuck the ball and run, he would run maybe more than you like and not slide, but he put his head down and thought he was going to run over somebody."

"I don't know that in all my years of evaluating quarterbacks I ever saw somebody that was capable of throwing on the move as accurately as he was," Bengals offensive coordinator Bob Bratkowski added.

Palmer could have easily pulled an Eli Manning, who told the San Diego Chargers before the 2004 draft not to select him because he didn't want to play for them. But Palmer saw through the Bengals' league-worst 55-137 record (.286) from 1991-2002. He saw the brilliant receivers in Chad Johnson and Peter Warrick, the veteran offensive line anchored by tackles Willie Anderson and Levi Jones, the bruising running of Rudi Johnson and a defense that is sure to improve.

Palmer is where he is today because

his father, an insurance executive, took a job on the East Coast when Carson was in high school. Bill chose to commute because Carson had a better chance of getting a college scholarship playing in California instead of Connecticut.

"It was a strain on them to live apart, but it was all out of love," Palmer said. "They loved me and that was a sacrifice they were willing to make."

Learning from their sins of the past when they forced Klingler and Smith into the lineup as rookies when they weren't ready, the Bengals allowed Palmer to learn the NFL ropes as a rookie behind Jon Kitna, who was the only quarterback to take every snap (1,078) for his team in 2003.

Lewis announced Palmer as the starter on March 1, then spent the remainder of the offseason building the team around him. Palmer doesn't have to carry the team, just lead it. "I'm the type of learner who needs to experience things," Palmer said. "I can't just sit in a room and look at plays on a chalk board. I need to be on the field and execute them."

Critics, of course, blame Kitna's demotion on the politics of the NFL. They contend the only reason for Palmer's elevation is money—after all, the club has millions invested in him, and it's time for the payoff to begin. The critics are correct in the sense that the team isn't paying Palmer a king's ransom to sit a second straight season. But they are wrong to think Palmer isn't ready.

Palmer has the ability to hold the ball that extra split second and rifle it into small openings in the defense. That's what makes him the best quarterback on the roster, the one who will ignite the vertical passing game, the one who gives the team the best chance to win.

"He can be the best that ever played the game," Kitna said. "When he went against the first team in practice last year for the scout team, you saw some amazing things. Physically, his talent is unbelievable. The way he throws the ball is phenomenal. The hard thing nowadays is: There's not much patience for people anymore. I'm going to do everything I can to make sure he's as ready as possible every Sunday. I'm excited to see him play."

(Palmer, 24, enters the second year of a six-year contract worth as much as $49 million. He received a $10 million signing bonus, with another $4 million bonus due in 2005 at the club's option. He married his college sweetheart, Shaelyn Fernandes, a goalie for the USC women's soccer team, at Pebble Beach, California, in 2003. Palmer's brother, Jordan, is a sophomore quarterback at Texas-El Paso.)

> **He can make every throw. He reaches the whole field. The worst thing we can do is have him think so much that his physical skills don't show.**
>
> **—QBs coach Ken Zampese**

261

The Man

¶Marvin Lewis, head coach (2003-present)

The exhaustive 16-day search ended on January 14, 2003, at the Grand Hotel Marriott Resort, Golf Club & Spa overlooking the shimmering waters of Mobile Bay in Point Clear, Alabama. Marvin Lewis got the contract he wanted, reaching agreement with Bengals president Mike Brown on a five-year deal. What he lacked was Bengals attire. It was late afternoon on Tuesday of Senior Bowl Week and Bengals public relations director Jack Brennan needed to get a press event rolling because of the amount of interest from a news-hungry media. "Marvin didn't have any Bengal gear yet," Brennan said, "so I just lent him one of my short-sleeved polo shirts with the Bengal tiger head on it. Luckily, I had a couple packed." As Lewis muscled into the shirt, he made history as the club's first African-American head coach and only the eighth black head coach in NFL history.

His first words were enough to give long-suffering Bengals fans what they craved—hope. "It's all about winning," Lewis said. "Whatever it takes... I remember when that stadium rocked and they called it 'The Jungle,' and I think it can get back to that."

Before Paul Brown Stadium opened in 2000, there was Riverfront Stadium, "The Jungle" that housed the Super Bowl runner-up Bengals during the 1981 and 1988 seasons. On the day it was imploded (December 29, 2002), the Bengals imploded 450 miles away, falling 27-9 at Buffalo to end the worst season (2-14) in club history.

Head coach Dick LeBeau was fired the next day and Brown had a decision to make. He could resurrect Forrest Gregg in the person of tough-guy Tom Coughlin. He could also select Sam Wyche's clone in Mike "Inspector Gadget" Mularkey. In the end, Brown picked Lewis, long considered the league's No. 1 assistant coach.

Lewis had heard stories about Cincinnati being the NFL's Siberia, but coached in the same division with

Said Lewis, "We're not that far away from being where we want to be. We're going to become better professionals. And on Sunday, that's going to come out in how we play."

What separates you and gets you over the hump in the NFL is how you finish things. You want to start fast, but you've got to finish.

—Marvin Lewis

Cincinnati Bengals

263

the Bengals long enough to know that wasn't the case. "Ironically, it was the opposite of what people perceived and that was an attraction," he said. "Mike really wanted somebody to come in and run the football team and direct as much as they feel comfortable in directing."

Lewis, the former defensive coordinator of the Baltimore Ravens (1996-2001) and Washington Redskins (2002), broke into the league as linebackers coach of the Pittsburgh Steelers (1992-95). But first, he had to break out of Western Pennsylvania, where his parents—Marvin Sr. and Vanetta—taught him the value of hard work.

A native of McDonald, Pennsylvania, outside Pittsburgh, Lewis saw his father leave for work every day at Shenango, Inc., a facility on Neville Island that produced blast furnace coke. Marvin Sr.'s job was difficult and dangerous, his elbows throbbing from years of pounding a sledgehammer and chipping molds, coming home so sore he had to prop his elbows up on pillows to ease the pain.

Marvin Jr. got a taste of Shenango one summer break from school, working the coke battery where the ovens reached 2,800 degrees. He got too close once and felt his plastic safety goggles melting from the searing heat. "Nine weeks of hell," Lewis said. His parents were crushed when Marvin phoned home in 1978 and said he wanted to be a football coach.

"I said, 'What?' " Marvin Sr. said. "I was very upset. He had all the intelligence, which I didn't have. He got that from his mother. I was hoping for him to be an engineer or whatever, something other than like me in the mill. At the time, I said, 'How far can a black coach go?' "

Marvin Jr. explained his decision with words his father will never forget. "He said, 'Daddy, you go into that mill every day and you hate that job. I want to do what I love to do.' That was it."

So Marvin Jr. spent 22 years climbing the football coaching ladder—11 years as a college assistant and 11 as an NFL assistant—before walking into that crowded news conference at the Marriott. He had been a serious contender for head coaching jobs before, but the problem, one writer said, "was that Marvin wanted to change the furniture overnight." That made him a perfect fit in Cincinnati.

The Bengals have a monument to football financed by taxpayers, a state-of-the-art palace the club said it needed to be competitive, yet the performance on the field had gone from bad to worse. Then along came Lewis and, overnight, everything changed.

Talk about a breath of fresh air, Lewis is a 200-pound tic tac. He overhauled the coaching staff, beefed up the personnel department, oversaw a $300,000 renovation of the weight room, scheduled Friday West Coast trips, signed his No. 1 pick before the draft, and became relentlessly involved in the community.

By design, Brown stepped out of the spotlight and into the shadows, and Lewis adopted a "one voice" policy. His voice. Lewis became the sole provider of information on everything from player moves to injury updates. He doesn't have the title of general manager, but he sure is acting like one. Lewis places a monetary value on players, and the club's "salary capologists"—the husband-wife team of Troy and Katie Blackburn, Brown's daughter and son-in-law—work closely with Lewis to make sure everything fits.

Until 2003, Lewis' greatest accomplishment came during the 2000 season when the Super Bowl Champion Ravens set the NFL record for fewest points allowed in a 16-game season with 165. All he did his first season in Cincinnati was perform a miracle. Taking over a club beaten down by 12 straight seasons without a winning record, a squad that owned the league's worst mark of 55-137 (.286) in that span, Lewis had the Bengals in the playoff hunt until the final weekend of the season before they finished 8-8.

Holding a shovel, symbolic of the team's work ethic, Lewis bawled like a baby in the sanctuary of the locker room after the Bengals upset 9-0 Kansas City, 24-19, on November 16, a moment captured by NFL Films.

"The one I'm most thankful for is Mike Brown," Lewis said in awarding the club president a game ball, "because he's endured a lot for you guys. He means it for you guys."

It's a lot to expect an inexperienced quarterback to reach the playoffs, but with Carson Palmer's talent and ever-improving supporting cast, the Bengals should end the league's longest playoff drought soon.

"We're no longer playing for respectability," Lewis said. "We're playing to be a champion. There is a certain aura of ineptitude that has been erased. People don't ever have to have that perception again."

(Lewis, 45, became the Bengals' ninth head coach January 14, 2003, replacing Dick LeBeau, who was fired after compiling a 12-33 record. Lewis attended Fort Cherry High School, the same school that produced San Diego Chargers head coach Marty Schottenheimer. Lewis and wife, Peggy, have two children, daughter Whitney, 19, and son Marcus, 14.)

> **He's all business. He knows where he's going and he knows how he's going to get there. If you're going to help him get there, fine. If not, he doesn't want to see you around.**
>
> **—defensive end Justin Smith**

Author Ludwig (left) and fellow staffer Marty Williams in the company of greatness—The Grand Old Man himself.

Chick Ludwig, an award-winning sports writer who has worked at the *Dayton Daily News* for 25 years, is the dean of the Bengals beat writers. He is chairman of the Cincinnati Chapter of the Pro Football Writers of America, the Bengals correspondent for *The Sporting News,* and serves on the 39-man selection committee for the Pro Football Hall of Fame. In 2002, Ludwig captured first place in the enterprise features category of the PFWA writing contest for his 50-part project, *The Rivalry,* chronicling the history of the Cincinnati Bengals-Cleveland Browns games. A native of Cincinnati, Ludwig graduated from The Ohio State University in 1976 with a Bachelor of Arts degree in Journalism.